CHILDREN'S PARTIES

CHILDREN'S PARTIES

JULIET MOXLEY

Photographs by Marie-Louise Avery

TED SMART

A TED SMART Publication

1 3 5 7 9 10 8 6 4 2

First published in the United Kingdom in 1993 by
Ebury Press, Random House, 20 Vauxhall Bridge Road,
London SW1V 2SA

Random House Australia (Pty) Limited
20 Alfred Street, Milsons Point, Sydney
New South Wales 2061, Australia

Random House New Zealand Limited
18 Poland Road, Glenfield
Auckland 10, New Zealand

Random House South Africa (Pty) Limited
PO Box 337, Bergvlei, South Africa

Random House UK Limited Reg. No. 954009

A CIP catalogue record for this book is available
from the British Library.

Editor Emma Callery
Design Roger Daniels
Food Stylist Janet Smith
Illustrator Kate Simunek

ISBN 0 09 182151 7

Typeset in Franklin Gothic ITC
by BMD Graphics, Hemel Hempstead
Printed and bound in Italy
by New Interlitho S.p.a., Milan

The Publishers and the Author would like to thank
the following people:

Pelikan UK Ltd for supplying fabric paints and pens
Dylon for supplying fabric pens, puffy and glitter
paint
Ells and Farrier for supplying beads and sequins
Paper Chase for supplying streamers and paper
Marie-Lou Avery for the photographs
Lucy Tizard for assisting
Jill Sheridan for the party games
Janet Smith for the food
Elna for the loan of their sewing machine
Ray the butcher for his astroturf
Cecilie Halvorson, Monica Syversen,
Rachel Collins, Karin Werstrom, Diana Hallstrom,
Sian Murphy, Anna Ashford for making props
Jay and Saha Haworth, Jack, Oliver, Jessica and
Alice Moxley, Anna and Christina Ashford, Carlene
Mills, Zander, Oliver Fare, Ping and Gee Lou,
Katherine, Edward and Anthony Saunt, Sophie and
Oliver Hallstrom, Sian Murphy, Maria Dunn,
Aitchee Jenkins, and Amy Bridge for being such
wonderful and co-operative models.

This book is dedicated to the deaf in the hope that
those who hear will listen, and not isolate them
further.

Contents

Introduction

This book is full of ideas for party giving; there are themes, recipes, games, costumes and suggestions for decorating rooms and tables and invitations. My qualifications for writing such a book are that I am a working mother with four children ranging in age from 1½ to 13 years, and we have held numerous parties in our house over the years. I know what a nerve-wracking experience it can be. This book gives some guidelines to successful party giving.

Two of the major concerns when holding a party are time and money. I have borne both in mind when writing this book. Although most of the costumes and decorations use household rubbish, re-cycled sheets, curtains and clothes, and are inexpensive, they do take a little time to make. Many of the props and backdrops, however, can be made by a family team, which can be fun and speed up the process of manufacture. With time in mind I have also included some quick ideas for costumes.

Every party featured here has some recipes to go with the theme, but these are just starting points and can be interchanged between parties. If your time is limited do not feel obliged to make party food – you do not have to make the food to have a successful party. You can use entirely shop-bought, instant food or all homemade items, or a combination of the two.

The games are chosen with particular themes in mind, but they too can be chopped and changed around. I have indicated throughout which games are particularly suitable for younger or older children, and those which are quiet and those which are boisterous.

Use this book as a handbook to fit in with your lifestyle. If you are very busy, don't try to make everything, rather try to rope in other willing hands to help, however young they are. Even little ones can hold a paint brush and they love making papier-mâché.

Forward planning

Before starting, you need to decide how many children you wish to have to the party, and where to hold it. You may wish to hold a joint party with another family and perhaps hire a school or church hall. If you do this, remember to check on names if both children are in the same class at school or you may duplicate.

Although the party is being held for your child, who should of course be consulted, do not be bullied into inviting more children than you feel you can cope with or have space for. If you can avoid it, do not attempt to throw a children's party alone. Enlist any friends willing to act as helpers on the day of the party. As a rule it is a good idea to invite an adult along

Venue

● If the party is being held at home, clear a room so there is enough room for games and moving around. If you are having an entertainer, decide upon a place where (s)he can set up for his/her performance and have a place for him/her to change.

● If planning an outside party, do not assume the weather will be good. Have an alternative place to hold the party if it rains.

● Make sure the children know where they can go and which places are out of bounds. Make sure every child knows where there is a toilet. Have a place to put coats and possessions.

● If you are hiring an outside venue, book

ahead as a place can often be booked out months in advance. Write to confirm the booking and two or three days before ring and confirm the time and date of the party. In this way the management have no excuse for double booking or forgetting you.

● Before booking a room go to see it. Check that there is adequate and safe lighting and heating. Find out whether there are tables and chairs and if they are suitable for the age of child you are inviting. Can they be cleared away for playing games? If you need to prepare or store food, is there somewhere to do this? Are the toilet facilities near and are they clean?

Different Requirements for Different Ages

This is a rough guide to what to expect from children of certain ages. It is not a hard and fast set of rules, they are just observations and you may find that your children are different.

1-year-olds Parties for 1-year-olds are as much for the proud parents as for the child. It might be a party with friends and grandparents, brothers and sisters. Pick a time of day when your child is not going to be asleep so he or she can appreciate it. If you are inviting small friends, each one will be accompanied by an adult so they will need to be taken into consideration when catering. Presents should be appropriate, but the wrapping paper will probably be of most interest to a 1-year-old.

2-year-olds Most 2-year-olds will want their Mum or Dad at a party. They will like being with other children but will not yet be ready for organized games. Two-year-olds like dancing, so put on some music. Have lots of toys around for children to play with. Keep the party short, an hour to an hour-and-a-half will be plenty.

3-year-olds can play short games. Their attention span is short but they do enjoy parties and will interact with one another at this age. Most of them are confident without Mum or Dad but you should have plenty of adults around to help with visits to the loo, washing hands and for hugs when someone falls over.

4-year-olds This is the best age for birthday parties. Children are enthusiastic and receptive and they tend to be cooperative and relate well to other children. The only danger at this age is overstimulation; too many activities and a party going on too long and the children will become fractious and irritable.

5-year-olds At this age self-conciousness can set in. Some children become very concerned with what is happening to their new-found prizes, party hats or cake. To counteract this, give each child a bag with his/her name written on it at the beginning of the party.

6-year-olds A 6-year-old will probably want to help in the preparation of the party. Cutting, gluing and painting skills can be put to good use making invitations and props. Six-year-olds have lots of energy and this should be taken into account when devising party games — allow lots of room to move.

7-year-olds are cooperative and understand about rules of games. It is at this age that leaders are beginning to emerge and this can be used to advantage by having team games, but make sure that no children get left out.

8-year-olds At this age co-ed parties are difficult as children prefer to have a party with just their own sex. This preference for their own sex can start earlier than 8 years and it is up to the parent to take this into consideration when inviting guests. Often children of this age want an outing as their party; ten-pin bowling, swimming, or a visit to a wax works followed by birthday tea at home is often the best treat.

9-year-olds are often very competitive and need to show off. Team games are good for this age as are any games which can show off mental or physical skills. Keep regrouping teams so that no one child can be picked on for a team not winning.

10-year-olds Ask any teacher and they will tell you, 10-year-olds are wonderful. They are enthusiastic and responsive and not too critical. They will want to make the party a success.

11- and 12-year-olds This age is difficult as there is conflict between the sexes, girls mature earlier than boys and therefore think boys of their own age are babyish. Boys tend to show off and to be rude. Rebellion often sets in and it is probably better to have an outing party with fewer numbers of the same sex than a conventional party.

Some pre-teen children like to have a few friends to stay for the night or to camp in the garden in a tent or even to have a disco party. If you choose a theme such as the fifties, sixties or seventies this will help to ease the atmosphere as they admire and laugh at one another's costumes and outfits.

with each child for 1- and 2-year-old children and for older children one adult for every eight to twelve children. If you have enough help and enough space, at the end of the day it doesn't matter how many children you invite. If you end up with more children than you have chairs for have a picnic party on the floor.

Invitations

Send out your invitations about three weeks before the party as this gives people time to schedule the party and to reply to you. If your child's birthday is in the middle of the holidays when lots of people will be away, have it at another time.

Make a list of your guests with their phone numbers and addresses. Tick off each guest as they reply so that you know who is coming and who isn't. Ring those people who haven't replied three days before the party to find out if they are coming.

When you write your invitations make sure that the wording is very clear and that the date, venue, starting time, and time for collection are all known. If the party is being held at a place other than your home, make sure that this is clear on the invitation.

If the party is a swimming or gym party make sure that children know, so that they can dress appropriately. (NOTE: For a swimming party ask the children to already be changed into their swimming gear as this will save a great deal of time at the beginning of the party.)

If you don't have time to make lots of invitations, make one, photocopy it and colour by hand. Before making the invitations, buy some envelopes and cut the card for the invitations to fit them.

The order of the party

The order in which you do things may depend on the venue and whether the party is indoors or outdoors, but as a rule it is a good idea to start with a warm-up game which children can join in as they arrive. Then have some more games, any entertainment you are having, the birthday tea and cake, and then a quiet game before going home. When and whether to open presents can also become a problem particularly if everyone arrives at the same time. Most children who have chosen a present like to see their friend open it. So do open presents at the party if you can. Make sure you know who has given what. Parents have different opinions about saying thank you and/or writing thank you letters. I feel that if a child has said thank you there is no need to make him/her write and say it again.

Where people sit at the birthday tea is of great importance to your child so let him/her choose where (s)he will sit and who will sit next to him/her. When you bring in the birthday cake, don't forget to bring the matches and have a camera ready.

Swag Bags

Different people have different opinions as to whether or not to give going home presents to guests. This can work out very expensive. In some homes a piece of birthday cake and a balloon are sufficient, especially if children have won little prizes throughout the party. An alternative idea is to have a lucky dip. Wrap up small individual presents and put them in a box of shredded tissue and each child can dive in and pick out one present.

Entertainers

Entertainers are usually popular but they are not cheap and as long as one has plenty of good entertainment in the form of games, they are not necessary. There is no point in having an entertainer for children under the age of 3, and at 3 and 4 for only a very short time as the children's attention span is limited.

The best way to find an entertainer is through word of mouth, as there is nothing like personal recommendation. Most good entertainers will need to be booked up in advance so ring and then write confirming the booking with the age of the child, the date, the time, and the venue. Ring two or three days before to check that the entertainer is turning up and still have a contingency plan in case (s)he doesn't. (S)he may catch a cold, break a leg or just get lost. Have a video film or standby games ready just in case.

When booking, check exactly what you are getting for your money. Is it just entertainment or does (s)he give prizes or help with the tea? Will (s)he give balloons? Above all, is his/her show going to entertain your age of child?

If you don't have enough chairs for your show the children can sit on the floor or on cushions.

Behaviour

There are three groups of people to consider when having a birthday party: the child whose birthday it is, the guests, and the siblings. The behaviour of all of them can make or break a party. The person whose birthday it is will have anticipated this day for a long time. It is a day when he/she is the special, chosen one. Nothing should be allowed to spoil this day. But even though it is your child's birthday, (s)he should know how to greet his/her guests, how to say thank you for presents and not to forget to say thank you for coming.

If the party is being held in the afternoon and there is much preparation to be done it may be a good idea for a partner or friend to take the child off somewhere until the time for the party. For younger children, a rest may be in order before the party commences.

Brothers and sisters are usually jealous of the attention given to the birthday boy or girl. It is important that these feelings are talked about. If you tell them that they will be the important one, the one receiving the presents on their birthday, this will help the situation.

Safety First

● Never give children under the age of 3 years peanuts.
● Do not leave any cleaning fluids, aspirins, etc. or anything small enough to swallow anywhere near toddlers.
● Never have open fires when children are rushing around, especially in flouncy full party dresses.
● For young children, put a stairgate up.
● Keep a first aid kit with you and the list of parents' numbers in case of emergency.
● Do not have matches or the knife for the birthday cake on the table.

Another ploy is to give each sibling a task to perform at the party. For example, they could hang up coats or be in charge of the music or props for games.

Parties tend to bring out the best and worst in behaviour so if a child is usually a bad loser, (s)he may be more so in a highly charged, often competitive, party situation. Some children feel that they always have to be winning. If you have one of these at your party, give him/her a job to do after (s)he has obviously won a game; for example, let him/her be a judge at musical statues.

Shy guests can also be a problem, sometimes they can help you with the food until perhaps they feel confident enough to join in with the games. Sometimes they may just like to be left alone to play with your child's toys, until they feel a little more relaxed. If a child is obviously miserable, contact his/her parents. Parties are supposed to be fun not a chore.

Try to introduce games where everyone can win a small prize; for example, pack a sweet or trinket beween layers in pass the parcel. Some games, however, involve children being 'out' while the game continues. This can allow for disruptive behaviour so have alternative games for them to do. For example, guessing the number of jelly beans in a jar. The nearest to the score gets the jelly beans to take home. Another good game is sucking chocolate beans up with straws from a plate, no hands allowed. You get to eat the chocolate beans you pick up.

Party Basics

Salt Dough

Salt dough is inexpensive and easy to make and once baked will last for years. It is a wonderful material for making party props and decorations. It can be painted and then varnished. The dough has been used for the Christmas Party (see page 114) and it can be used for many other parties for making pretend food and small models.

1 cup salt
1 cup warm water
3 cups plain flour
1tsp glycerine
water colours or poster paints
clear varnish

1 Dissolve the salt in warm water, this will make the dough smoother.
2 Sieve the flour into a bowl and add glycerine.
3 Pour in the salt water solution stirring all the time.
4 When the mixture is fairly stiff take it out and knead it as if making bread. The dough is then ready to model.

BAKING
Leave the dough to stand over night if possible. Start cooking the dough at a very low temperature, approximately 100°C (200°F, gas mark ¼) for 30 minutes. Then gradually turn the oven up to 150°C (300°F, gas mark 2) as the dough firms up and leave until the dough is quite solid. The time that this takes depends on the thickness of the item and its size. Small Christmas tree decorations, for example, may take only 30 minutes, while larger pieces such as garlands may take 3-4 hours.

DECORATING
The dough must be completely dry before beginning to decorate. Paint with water colours or poster paints. When the paint is dry, varnish with a clear varnish. Always varnish both sides of the dough as this will ensure it is well sealed and cannot grow mould.

For a natural look, paint each piece with egg white before baking and do not paint afterwards. The result is a warm, rich, golden brown.

MAKING CHRISTMAS TREE DECORATIONS
1 Make a quantity of salt dough and roll it out as if it were pastry. using special shaped pastry cutters (stars, Father Christmas, sheep, etc.), cut out the shapes and place them on tin foil or a baking tray.
2 Make holes near the top of each shape with a skewer.
3 Bake in the oven as described to the left.
4 When cooked, remove from the oven, allow to cool, and decorate with water colours or poster paints.
5 Varnish and then leave to dry.
6 Thread ribbon through the holes to hang from a tree.

Papier-Mâché

Papier-Mâché is the ideal substance for making models, costumes and props. It can be worked on a balloon, on chicken wire, onto cardboard and plastic containers, or it can be moulded into simple shapes. Papier-mâché is very simple to decorate and a final coat of varnish ensures it will last.

All it is is basically paper and glue. For all the props in this book I have used newspaper and wallpaper paste. You can, however, use PVA diluted 50 : 50 with water. This gives a very strong finish, or you can use flour and water paste.

To make flour and water paste, you need 1 mug of water and 3 mugs of flour. In a saucepan, mix a little of the water with the flour until you have a smooth paste and then add the rest of the water slowly, stirring all the time. Heat the mixture until it boils and let it simmer until the paste thickens. Turn the heat off and use when cold.

To papier-mâché
1 Rip newspaper into strips about 2.5cms (1in) wide. Dip the paper into glue and then squeeze off the excess between thumb and forefinger.
2 Apply the paper strips onto the base you are using. Work one layer at a time and allow to dry between layers. Five or six layers are usually enough for any project.
3 When dry, paint with a coat of white emulsion before decorating.

Costumes

From three basic patterns you can make most fancy dress costumes you are ever likely to need. A tabard can be used for a red Indian dress, a Peter Pan, elf or pixy, a soldier, or even a painting smock. A cloak can be for a wizard, a witch, a knight, a lady, Little Red Riding Hood, a conjuror. An all-in-one may be an animal, a racing driver, a clown, or a space man.

To make a jacket or trousers use the top or bottom of the all-in-one pattern and add a generous seam allowance at the waist or hem to allow for alterations.

Skirts are tubes of material with an elasticated top which adjusts to the size of the wearer.

CLOAK

For a photographic step-by-step sequence see page 72.

1 To make a full cloak you will need a large square of fabric: 135cms² (54ins²). Fold the square in half and place against the child's shoulder; this will show how long the cloak will be. Open out the material.

2 Fold the square in half and half again.

3 Draw a small curve on the corner with the folds for the neck and a large curve on the opposite corner for the hem.

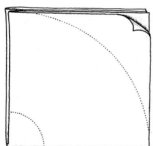

4 Cut along the curves.

5 Open out the material. You will have a large circle with a hole in the centre. Cut a straight line from the small circle to the large one. This is the front of the cloak.

6 Fold over 6mm (¼in) of the raw edges and hem to neaten. Add ribbon ties at the neck.

7 If you wish to add a collar, measure the length of the neck and cut a piece of fabric this length plus 12mm (½in) seam allowance, by double the depth you wish the collar to be.

8 Sew the collar onto the neck along one long side of the collar, right sides together. Fold the collar down and sew the other long side onto the neck hiding any raw edges. Neaten the edges of the collar by turning them in and sewing by hand.

9 To make a hood, cut a smaller circle (68cm [27ins]) of fabric and cut it in half. With right sides facing, sew the two halves together down their straight edge. Sew a piece of ridgeline or boning along the inside of the seam. This will make the hood stand out round the face. Stitch together and gather the double thickness of the semi-circle and sew it onto the neck line.

SIMPLE CLOAK

Instead of using a circle, this method uses a rectangle of fabric. Make a channel along one of the narrow ends to carry elastic or draw string.

Neaten the bottom and sides with a hem or running stitch. Fasten the cloak with a button or draw string. For a knight, appliqué a shield on the back.

TABARD

1 To calculate the amount of fabric needed, measure from the shoulder to the knee, add 5cms (2ins) for seam allowances and double the measurement.

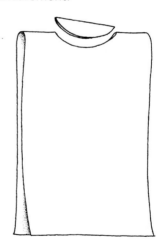

2 Cut your length of fabric, fold it in half and cut a hole large enough to fit over the child's head. If you wish, cut a further slit down the front of about 10cms (4ins) and make holes either side of the slit for lacing.

3 Neaten round the neck and the sides of the tabard. You can sew up the sides if you wish, but leave lots of room for the arms to move easily.

4 If you are not sewing up the sides, sew on ribbon or bias binding tape at the sides and stitch to the reverse side of the fabric.

ALL-IN-ONE

From this pattern you can make every conceivable kind of animal as well as making a clown and a spaceman.

The pattern fits a 4- to 6-year-old but can be enlarged as indicated. Each piece incorporates a 15mm (⅝in) seam allowance.

1 Enlarge the pattern given here onto dressmakers' grid paper or photocopy it. Check that the arms and legs fit your child.

2 Cut out two fronts, two backs, and two arms for each costume.

3 With right sides facing, sew the two fronts together as far as the dot.

4 Sew in velcro or a zip down the rest of the front seam.

5 With right sides facing, sew the two backs together down the centre back seam. If making an animal, leave a gap for the tail.

6 Sew the darts on the shoulder seams. Pin the sleeves to the edges of the arm holes front and back. Sew into position.

7 Sew down all the seams.

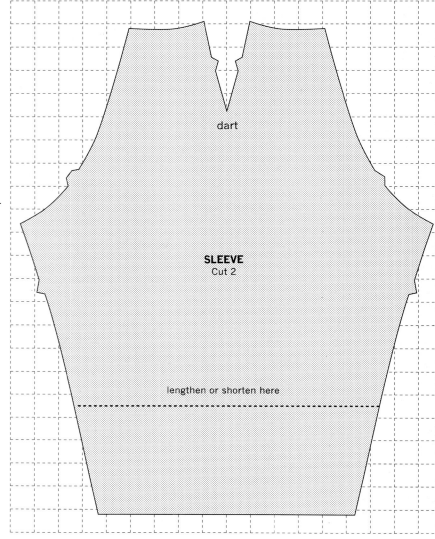

dart

SLEEVE
Cut 2

lengthen or shorten here

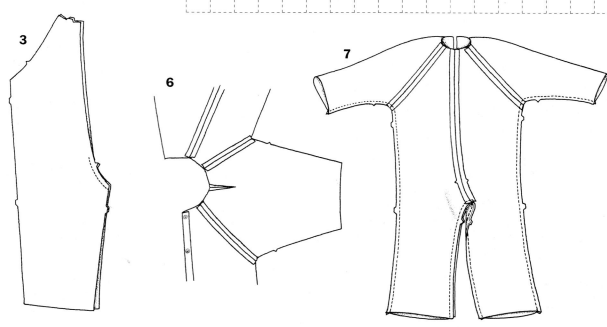

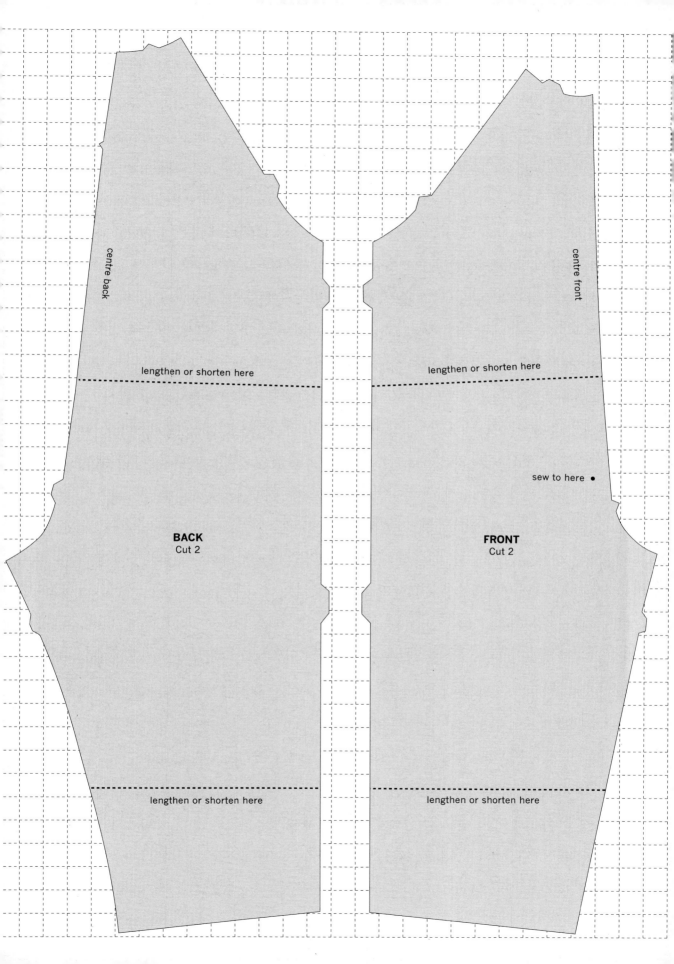

Hoods

To make the rabbit, chick, teddy bear, tiger and leopard hoods featured in this book, use the pattern pieces below. Whichever animal hood you decide to make, choose the correct colour fake fur and then follow the instructions below.

1 Using 2.5cms (1in) squared paper, draw and cut out the relevant pattern pieces. Each piece has a 15mm (⅝in) seam allowance included in the outline.

2 Cut two hood shapes from fur, two ears from fur and a further two ears from lining fabric or felt. For a chick, cut two beaks from orange felt and an additional beak shape from interfacing.

3 Sew the darts on each piece, right sides together, and then sew the two head pieces together around the curved seam – again, with right sides together. Ensure that you leave space to fit the hood over the child's head.

4 To make the ears, with right sides together, stitch the pleats and then sew the felt linings to the fur ears. Turn right sides out and then stitch the ears into place as indicated below.

5 For the chick, iron the interfacing onto one side of one of the beaks and then sew the beaks together with the interfacing sandwiched between them. Sew the beak into place as on the photograph on page 17.

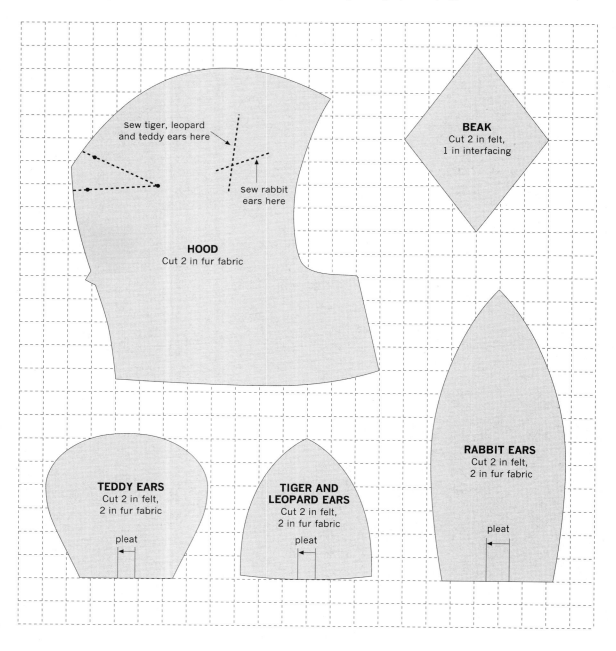

Sew tiger, leopard and teddy ears here

Sew rabbit ears here

HOOD
Cut 2 in fur fabric

BEAK
Cut 2 in felt, 1 in interfacing

RABBIT EARS
Cut 2 in felt, 2 in fur fabric

TEDDY EARS
Cut 2 in felt, 2 in fur fabric

pleat

TIGER AND LEOPARD EARS
Cut 2 in felt, 2 in fur fabric

pleat

pleat

14

Party Food

WORKING OUT QUANTITIES

It is better to over cater then under cater. You can always use leftovers for meals, snacks and school lunches. Leftover sandwiches can be frozen and toasted or fried, or just used later. Don't open all the packets of crisps or savoury biscuits at once, as these are difficult to re-use as they get soggy.

As younger children are sometimes accompanied by their mothers and/or fathers who may also want to eat, don't forget to cater for them as well.

Here is a rough guide to quantities. Of course, some children will eat more than this and others less.

For each child:

1 small packet of crisps or biscuits
4 cocktail sausages
4 bite-sized sandwiches
4 cheese straws
3 sweet biscuits
1 piece of pizza
1 piece birthday cake
a jelly and /or ice cream

The quantities given in the recipes in this book are designed to cater for a party of 10 children.

Basic Recipes

Recipes containing eggs in this book require Size 2 eggs to be used. Some of the recipes use raw eggs. If you are feeding very young children it is advisable not to make these because of the possible risk of salmonella.

CAKE MIX

110g (4oz) soft margarine
110 (4oz) caster sugar
2 eggs
110g (4oz) self-raising flour
1 tbsp water

Pre-heat oven to a temperature of 200°C (400°F, gas mark 6)
Cream together the fat and sugar. Add the beaten eggs, a little at a time to prevent curdling. Add the sieved flour and the water if the mixture is too dry. Bake in paper cases, or as otherwise suggested, for 15 minutes.

THINGS TO REMEMBER FOR THE TEA

- Do not pour drinks before the children have sat down or you are guaranteed to have spillages.
- Always have some non-fizzy drinks if you are serving Coke and lemonade as many children prefer non-carbonated drinks.
- Remember to make tea for the helpers, other parents, and the entertainer if there is one.

GLACÉ ICING

225g (8oz) icing sugar
2 tbsp warm water
colouring, as required

1 Sift the sugar into a bowl and add the warm water. Beat well until smooth and thick enough to coat the back of a wooden spoon.
2 If necessary, add a little extra liquid. If you add too much liquid, simply sift in more sugar to achieve the required consistency. To colour glacé icing, add a few drops of the chosen food colouring and beat in well.

BUTTER ICING

2 egg whites
110g (4oz) icing sugar
150g (5oz) butter, softened

1 Place the egg whites and sugar in a bowl over a pan of simmering water. Whisk for 5-7 minutes until the mixture is thick and white. Remove from the heat and continue whisking until cool.
2 Beat the butter until fluffy, then fold in the egg whites and sugar mixture.

SHORTCRUST PASTRY

110g (4oz) plain flour
salt
50g (2oz) margarine
2 tbsp water

1 Sift the flour and a pinch of salt into a bowl. Add the fat to the flour in small pieces.
2 Using your fingertips rub the fat into the flour. Add water and mix the whole together. Wrap the pastry in cling film and leave to chill in the fridge for 20 minutes.

A Spring-time Party

Spring-time with its blossom and flowers, lambs and new life is always a good excuse for a party especially after a cold grey winter. Your spring party may be specifically to celebrate Easter in which case decorate paper and real eggs with paper flowers; make Easter bonnets laden with paper flowers and ribbons, and dress the children as chicks, lambs or rabbits.

Costumes

- For a bunny head (see previous page), use the hood pattern on page 14 and make it in white fur with long ears attached.
- The bunny tail is made from a white cotton wool ball, pompom, or circle of fake fur with a gathered line of running stitches round the edge.
- Make a lamb hood (see previous page) from woolly fake fur, and its tail from a long piece of fake fur.
- A chicken hood is made from yellow fake fur with a yellow/orange beak attached.
- Make an Easter crown from fake flowers wired together.

Easter Hoods

Animal hoods (see instructions on page 14) are particularly suitable for spring parties. Whichever animal hood you decide to make, choose the correct colour fake fur (white for a rabbit and yellow for a chick) and then cut two hood shapes (see outline on page 14). In addition, for a rabbit: cut two long white ears and two pink felt linings. For a chick: cut two orange beaks and a piece of interfacing.

Below: for table decorations, decorate eggs and make simple nests for food containers.

Party Games

PAINTING EGGS

This is a good activity with which to start the party so that all the children are occupied while everyone is arriving.

Props Boil enough eggs so that all children have one to decorate (plus some extra for breakages), wax crayons (if younger children), wool, string (for older children), saucepans with different coloured dye – red water (from boiled beetroot), yellow water (from onions), blue water (from red cabbage). If you are entertaining older children, you can always try blowing eggs. You do this by making tiny holes in the top and bottom of the eggs and gently blowing out the innards through one of the holes.

How to proceed Allow each child to select an egg and to decorate it. If using wax crayons, encourage the child to colour thick areas rather than thin patterns as this is more successful. Older children can wind string or thick thread round the egg fastening the ends securely. Once the desired pattern is complete, let the child select a colour dye and place the egg in the appropriate saucepan. Leave the eggs in the dye until near the end of the party. Remove eggs from the dye and allow to dry. If string/wool has been used, gently remove with scissors and the pattern becomes apparent.

HUNT THE EGG

Props Basket/other container per child, variety of shop-bought small eggs – chocolate, sugar coated, wrapped in various shiny papers.

To play Hide the eggs in the house or garden and set the children various tasks such as 'Find three speckled eggs', or 'Find four eggs wrapped in blue paper and three wrapped in silver paper', or 'Find ten eggs each of which must be a different colour'. (The children now have something to take home at the end of the party.)

ANIMAL CHARADES

This is a team game for younger children which requires three or more players per team. It is important to stress that no sound effects are allowed.

Props List of animals for each team, pen. It is useful to have different lists for each team as it can become rather noisy and players pick up hints from others.

To play One child elects to begin and is told which animal to be. (S)he acts as the animal to his/her other team members. The team member who guesses correctly goes quickly to the organiser, whispers the name of the animal and if correct is then given another for the team to guess. The team who wins is the one who finishes the whole list first.

Decorating Easter Eggs

1 Place a variety of small leaves in water to help them stick to the eggs. When well wetted through, smooth a leaf onto an egg.

2 To hold the leaf in place, wrap a piece cut from some tights around the egg. Tie a knot in the tights to keep in place. Then mix some fabric dye according to the manufacturer's instructions.

3 Gently lower the eggs into a simmering saucepan of the dye for 20 minutes. Drain under the cold tap and remove the tights and leaf. An imprint of the leaf will be left.

Party Food

The food which springs to mind when thinking about Easter is eggs, usually the chocolate ones. Here, there is a variation on the egg theme: marbled eggs in a nest of noodles.

RABBIT SANDWICHES

1 loaf of bread, brown or white
butter
egg mayonnaise (see Eggy Caterpilllars,
   page 44)
cress, chopped
rabbit-shaped cutter or
   template made from card
carrot, sliced

1 Spread the bread with butter. Make the egg mayonnaise and spread this on the butter and add the chopped cress. Put the lid on the sandwich and leave in the fridge for an hour.
2 Cut off the crusts and stamp out the rabbit shapes. Garnish with a sliver of carrot as if the rabbit is eating it.

RABBIT CRUMPETS

1 carrot per person
1 crumpet per person
jar of cocktail onions
raisins
small can of
   sweetcorn
cheese

1 Peel the carrots and cut into slices. Use two slices per crumpet for ears. Trim them as necessary and place on the crumpet with a slight overlap.
2 Make bunny eyes from cocktail onions, a nose from a raisin, teeth from sweetcorn, and whiskers from slivers of carrot. Grate cheese over the face and then put under a hot grill until the cheese melts.

MARBLED EGGS IN A NOODLE NEST

1 egg per person
food colouring
ice cubes
250g (9oz) noodles

1 Put the eggs in cold water and boil for 3 minutes. Remove the eggs from the water and add 2 tsp food colouring to the water. Tap the eggs all over until the shell is crazed and return them to the water for a further 6 minutes.
2 Fill a bowl with cold water and add 3 or 4 ice cubes and a further tsp of food colouring. Plunge the eggs into the water and leave for a further 10 minutes.
3 Meanwhile, cook the noodles as instructed on the pack. Remove the eggs from the water and take off their shells. They should be clearly marbled. Place the strained noodles in a large bowl with the eggs on top.

PEAR RABBIT OR PERE RABBIT

1 tinned pear per
   person (makes
   two rabbits)
slivered almonds
raisins
carrots
lettuce
cottage cheese

1 Cut the pear in half lengthways to make a rabbit shape (the narrow end is the nose end). Cut a notch near the head end and insert two almond ears. Make a hole for the eyes and insert the raisins. Do the same for the nose. Make whiskers from tiny carrot wedges pushed into the sides of the rabbit face.
2 Place the rabbit on a bed of lettuce and add 1 tsp of cottage cheese to each to make a fluffy tail.

Fairies and Elves

Young children love fairyland. It is where dreams are made and wishes fulfilled. You can easily transform your home into fairyland with a few simple props. Make streamers from milk bottle tops and kitchen foil, string up your Christmas tree lights and make sure your fairies and elves join the best party in town!

Costumes

- For a pixy or elf outfit (see previous page), use a tabard of green felt (see page 11) with a zigzag hem with bells attached. Wear it with green or black tights and pixy boots and make a pointed green hat with a bell on the end.
- False ears can be made from papier-mâché (see page 10), sewn or stuck onto the sides of the elf's cap.
- For a fairy (see below) decorate a leotard with a netting skirt and sequins
- A full-length petticoat with a frilly nylon skirt can be decorated with glitter.
- Make wings from silver card edged with Christmas tinsel and attach them with two elastic straps coming over the shoulders.
- More wings can be made from netting stuck onto bent wire wing-shaped coat hangers or from metallic tissue lamé boned with ridgeline.
- A wand can be made from silver-sprayed dowelling and two star-shaped pieces or cardboard covered in glitter.

To Decorate a Fairy Dress

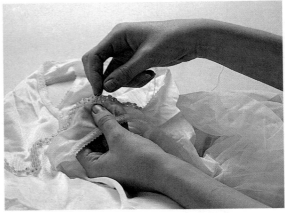

1 Sew or stitch sequins or diamanté onto the fairy dress.

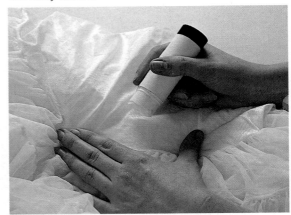

2 Either buy a petticoat with a net skirt or attach a netting petticoat to a vest or leotard. Spread glue along the edge of the petticoat.

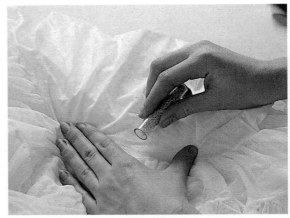

3 Making sure your work area is covered with paper, sprinkle glitter onto the glue. Shake the excess glitter onto the paper and put back in a jar. If there are any gaps in the glitter, re-stick and sprinkle on some more.

Room Decorations

Milk bottle tops strung together and hung around the room are the ideal decoration for a party such as this one. Or hang Christmas fairy lights on the walls, and also swags of white, pale blue or pink netting, adorned with sequins and glitter. Tie silver ribbon along the swags at intervals to brighten the netting. Cut stars from cardboard, cover them with glue and then sprinkle glitter all over them. Thread the stars onto gold or silver thread or ribbon and festoon your rooms.

Stars, toadstools and fairy sweets are ideal table decorations.

Party Games

WHAT CAN IT BE?

This activity can be ongoing and is useful right at the beginning while children are arriving. But if you prefer, it can also be played by everyone at the same time.

Props Two prizes (preferably with a loose connection to the party theme such as a wand, something fluorescent that glows, a book with fairies or elves as the subject matter), wrapping paper, string, sticky tape.

To Play Loosely wrap the prizes with five or six layers of paper. The children are going to guess what is inside. Each child in turn feels the parcel and is allowed to ask one question which will help to discover what is inside. Every time a child asks something which proves useful in this quest that child may remove one layer of wrapping. This continues until the last layer is removed and that player may keep the prize. If anyone wishes to make an educated guess, this can happen at any stage but it must fit the information already revealed. More or fewer layers of wrapping can be added depending on the age of the children.

PUFF BALL

Props Ping pong balls (one per team), large straws (one for each player), tape to act as a finishing line

To Play Divide players into teams which are lined up at one end of the room. Lie the tape on the floor at the other end of the room to mark the finish. Everyone is given a straw and the first person a ping pong ball. Once the signal to start has been given the first player has to blow the ping pong ball to the other end of the room and over the tape. (S)he must then pick up the ball, run back to his/her team and give the ball to the next player who then repeats the whole exercise. The first team to have all players complete this wins. Remember — the straw must not touch the ping pong ball at any stage.

SQUEAL ELF SQUEAL

This is the old traditional game 'Sqeak piggy squeak' which younger children find very amusing.

Props Cushion, scarf to be used as a blindfold

To Play Ask for a volunteer to be blindfolded. Once you have checked that the child cannot see, turn him/her round three times. The rest of the children then find a seat in the room and must keep very quiet. The blindfolded player is then handed a cushion and has to move round the room until (s)he finds a child on whose lap the cushion is placed. (S)he then sits on the cushion and says 'Squeal elf squeal' and must then wait for the player underneath to respond. The blindfolded child has to guess on whose lap (s)he is sitting. If the guess is correct these two then swap places, and if wrong (s)he continues to be blindfolded and tries again.

Party Food

Children relish holding parties in their magic fairy kingdom. Keep all the food gossamer light and fun. Wicked pixies and gnomes love to run away with the odd butterfly cake.

SAVOURY WANDS

Cheddar cheese, or similar
Twiglets/cocktail sticks

1 Cut the cheese into 12mm (½in) slices and make small stars using a star-shaped pastry cutter.
2 Make a hole in the edge of the cheese and insert a Twiglet/cocktail stick. If using cocktail sticks, the wands can be stuck into a half grapefruit for presentation.

STARRY SALAD

1 large potato, sliced thinly
2 slices Edam cheese
2 slices cooked ham
2 slices salami
1 large carrot, thinly sliced
cucumber
1 cos lettuce

1 Using a small star-shaped cutter, cut out stars from the potato. Steam for about 7 minutes, or until tender.
2 Using the same cutter, cut stars from the cheese, ham, salami, carrot and cucumber. Shred the cos lettuce. Arrange the starry ingredients on the lettuce bed.

BUTTERFLY CAKES

quantity cake mix (see page 15)
paper cake cases
glacé icing, coloured pink (see page 15)
jelly decorations, chopped
liquorice sticks, 100s and 1000s

Pre-heat the oven to a temperature of 200°C (400°F, gas mark 6)
1 Mix together the ingredients as on page 15 and bake in the paper cake cases for 15 minutes.
2 When cold, slice off the top of each cake as if it were an egg. Decorate the remaining top with the glacé icing and add the chopped jelly decorations.
3 Spread glacé icing over the sliced off tops, cut them in half and stick on the cakes to look like butterfly wings. Add the liquorice sticks and 100s and 1000s to decorate.

UPSIDE DOWN SWEET TOADSTOOLS

chocolate-coated marshmallow cakes
miniature chocolate swiss rolls
glacé icing, coloured white and green
 (see page 15)
1 packet chocolate beans

1 Lie the marshmallows upside down.
2 Cut the swiss rolls in half and, using the white glacé icing, stick the cut end of the roll onto the underside of the marshmallows.
3 Using the green glacé icing, draw lines on the underside of the toadstool and stick the chocolate beans around the stalk.

Table Decorations

Plates and mugs decorated for fairies and elves to eat and drink from are easily made. For the plates, cut one star shape, stick it to the centre of a blue plate and decorate between the stars with smaller, self-sticking stars. Decorate the paper mugs with silver stars. Stick small stars around straws. To decorate the food, stick two small stars around cocktail sticks and put these into the food.

Fairy toadstools make really attractive decorations for the centre of your table. Cut a circular piece of card from a cereal packet and stick a crumpled piece of paper to the top to make a dome shape. Papier-mâché over the whole (see page 10). The stem is made from a toilet roll centre stuck to the underside of the toadstool by strips of masking tape and then covered with papier-mâché. Decorate with emulsion paints and weigh down by sticking Plasticine in the middle of the toilet roll.

A Circus Party

Be a clown be a clown. Often party entertainers come dressed as clowns, so why not the guests themselves? Or even a weight lifter or trapeze artist. Swim suits can be decorated with sequins and large trousers held up by braces. Decorate plastic plates to look like clown faces and mugs to look like bodies.

Costumes

- Make a clown costume (see previous page) from an all-in-one pattern (see page 12) made from lots of bright fabrics. Cover it in ribbons, add patch pockets and a ribbon ruff collar.
- A clown hat can be made from a cardboard cone decorated with pompoms, or use a bowler hat decorated with children's tree decorations and pompoms, some of which are on pipe cleaners.
- Paint a clown face using face paints: make a big mouth and rosy cheeks.
- A ring master costume is easily adapted from an old tail jacket and a top hat.
- Be a weight lifter in a swim suit with a broom stick with balloons on either end.
- For an acrobat, wear a leotard decorated with sequins and diamanté.

False shoes for a clown can easily and quickly be made from card. Place a shoe on a large piece of card and draw an enlarged shoe shape in front and behind it. Cut out the large shoe shape and also cut a hole in the centre of the card for the foot to fit through. Paint the card whatever colour you choose – brown, white, black, a mixture – and then draw laces and a shoe tongue and paint on a patch. Make a second shoe in the same way and wear over ordinary shoes to the party.

A clown hat with a felt flower and pompoms can be made by either using an old bowler hat or buying a cheap one and decorating it by attaching coloured pompoms. To do this, sew pompoms onto coloured pipe cleaners, make a hole in the hat and push them through. Firmly stitch them in place on the inside of the hat. The flower can be made from felt and similarly sewn onto a pipe cleaner and then attached onto the hat. Bend the pipe cleaners so they stick out sideways.

Decorating Clown Mugs

1 Cut a bow tie from a piece of card. Decorate with stripes, stars or spots. Cut out buttons and decorate them.

2 Stick on the bow tie at the top of the mug and stick the buttons beneath it.

3 From some brightly coloured card, cut a pair of feet which are large enough to stick out from under the mug. Decorate them with spots or stripes. Stick to the underside of the mug.

4 Two completed mugs.

1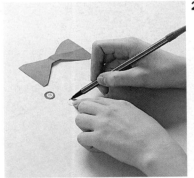

2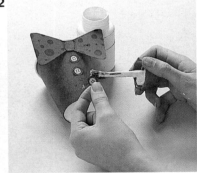

3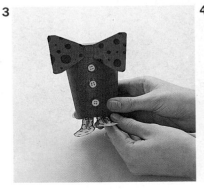

4

Party Games

HAT PASSING

This game is surprisingly difficult for younger children so I have included a simplified variation.

Props Enough hats for each child to wear one each, tape machine with music.

To Play Children, wearing their hats, stand in a circle facing the back of the child to their right. Play the music and let each child remove the hat from the head of the child in front. The hat is then placed on their own head and so on until the music stops. Do this several times so that everyone knows what to do. You then remove one hat and play begins. When the music stops this time the person without the hat is out. When there are only two children left, they should face each other. The winner is the child left wearing the hat.

If children are younger, throw the hats into a central area and when the music stops each child has to quickly pick up a hat and put it on. The child without one is out.

PASS THE PARCEL — (with a difference)

This is played in the opposite way to the traditional pass the parcel and does not require numerous layers of paper and string.

Props Prize wrapped as a normal gift with one layer of paper, (an idea would be to have a paperback book with a circus related story), a booby prize wrapped in the same way, tape recorder with music.

To Play Children are all seated in a circle. The two parcels are given to children on opposite sides of the circle. The parcels are passed in the same direction as each other until the music stops. Children holding the parcels when the music stops are out. This continues until two players are left. These two pass the parcels between them and open the one in their hands when the music stops. It is a good idea to have a note in the booby prize which says 'Thank you for being a good sport'.

Party Food

Circus food can range from animal-shaped biscuits and sandwiches to the bright colours of the big top and the large clown feet of your entertainers. You can even make your own popcorn to nibble in the interval between games.

CLOWN FEET BISCUITS

225g (8oz) plain
   flour
110g (4oz) butter
110g (4oz) caster sugar
1 tsp vanilla essence
1 egg, beaten
glacé icing, in various
   colours (see page 15)
glacé cherries
red liquorice laces

Pre-heat the oven to a temperature of 180°C (350°F, gas mark 4)
1 Mix together the flour and butter. Stir in the sugar and vanilla essence, add the egg and mix to a dough. Knead lightly and then wrap in cling film and chill in the fridge for an hour.
2 Roll out the dough, divide into smaller pieces and shape each one as if looking down on a shoe. Bake on a greased baking sheet for 12-15 minutes.
3 When cooled, add shoe-like patterns with glacé icing, add the glacé cherries and liquorice laces.

Table Decorations

Clown face plates which are brightly coloured are best, although white ones will do. To decorate them, draw eyes, mouths, noses, and anything else you can think of on the back of gummed paper squares. Cut them out, carefully colour or paint them and then stick onto the plates. Onto the outer edge of the plate, stick a hat, ruff or hair cut from card. If you want something more permanent, use ceramic paints to paint the face and then oven-bake to fix.

POPCORN

sunflower seed oil
a saucepan with a lid
1 packet popping corn
small boxes or margarine tubs painted or
   covered in brightly coloured paper
granulated sugar

1 Heat the oil in the pan. To test if it is hot enough, drop in one piece of corn: if it explodes the oil is hot enough. Add the rest of the corn (or the quantity stipulated on the packet) and quickly jam on the lid.
2 Agitate the pan over the heat until no more popping occurs. Turn off the heat and remove the pan. Pour the corn into the prepared tubs and sprinkle with sugar.

BIG TOP PIZZA

pizza bases, ready bought
tomato paste
red, yellow and
   green peppers
cheese

1 Cut one edge off each pizza base to form the roof of the big top and spread the whole with tomato paste.
2 Cover the base with tomato paste. Cut slices of red, yellow and green pepper and arrange them on the tent to form stripes. Add strips of cheese over the roof of the tent. Bake according to the instructions of the pizza base.

SUGARED CIRCUS PONIES AND ELEPHANTS

225g (8oz) packet puff pastry
1 egg, beaten
a little caster sugar
pony and elephant cutter (if not available, draw
   outlines on a piece of card and use as a
   template)

Pre-heat the oven to a temperature of 200°C (400°F, gas mark 6)
1 Roll the pastry into a very thin sheet. Brush with egg and sprinkle sugar on top. Cut out the pony and elephant shapes.
2 Bake on a dampened baking sheet for between 6 and 12 minutes.

A Valentine Party

Valentine parties are about love —
not just romantic love but friendship
and love between brothers and
sisters. The obvious symbol is
the heart. It is easy to draw
and can be used to decorate
costumes, walls and tables.
Other romantic images to
use for decorating are
cherubs and cupids.

Costumes

- Go-faster cupid wings can be made from card or wadding-filled lamé and stitched onto a headband (see right).
- Make a cupid costume (see previous page) from a wide tabard (see page 11) of white cotton or muslin with drawstring shoulders.
- A headdress is made by twisting ivy round and round. It could be sprayed gold or silver.
- Make wings for shoes and also put them on armbands which can be attached using velcro.
- Make a Valentine hat from a heart-shaped box painted red with heart-shaped chocolates stuck inside. Hold it on with a red ribbon.
- Wear a heart-shaped apron made from red material with a lace edge stitched onto it.

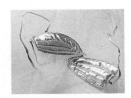

For cupid wings, draw a large wing-shape onto paper, cut it out and use as a pattern. Iron vylene onto the back of tissue lamé to strenghten it. Cut four wing shapes from the tissue lamé. Cut two lengths of boning to fit lengthways down the wings and sew onto the wrong side of two of the wings. With right sides facing, pin together an unboned and a boned wing and stitch three-quarters of the way around the edge. Turn the right sides out. Repeat with the other wing. Sew the wings onto a costume or tie around cupid's head (as illustrated on the previous page).

Party Games

BALLOON SQUEEZE

Here is a game that can be easily adapted, depending on the age group involved.

Props One balloon for each child and a few extra, tape recorder and music.

To Play Each child has a balloon which (s)he places between his/her knees. When the music plays, everyone must move in whichever way they wish taking care not to burst their balloons. When the music stops, everyone must stand very still keeping hold of their balloons between the knees. If there is any movement or a balloon is dropped or burst, that child is out.

For an older age group divide the children into two teams. The first member of each team has a balloon and again places it between the knees. Pass the balloon from one pair of knees to the next without dropping it or touching it by hand.

BLIND MAN'S BUFF

Children need to be warned to be quiet and calm when moving about for this game — partly because of safety and partly for the success of the game. Remove any objects that a child could harm him/herself with.

Props Scarf.

To Play One volunteer is blindfolded and is turned round three times to disorientate him/her. The other players have to move quietly round in a relatively small area while the blindfolded player tries to catch someone. Once someone is caught (s)he must stand still while hair, face, arms, etc. are felt so that the blindfolded child can guess who it is (s)he has captured. If the guess is correct these two change places and play starts again.

POSTMAN'S KNOCK

This is a must for a Valentine party and would be a good game with which to end. No props are needed and the children can play by themselves if you want to be getting things prepared for the end of the party.

To Play The children all sit round in a circle and are given a number. One child is the postman and has been waiting outside the room. The postman knocks at the door and the children shout 'Come in'. (S)he enters and has to call out a number. The child whose number it is has to go and kiss the postman and then go out of the room taking the place of that child. Children then re-number themselves before the new postman knocks at the door. Play continues in this way until the allocated time is up.

Making a Valentine Invitation

1 Cut a heart shape from cardboard and stick a larger heart shape cut from wadding to it.

2 Cut out a satin heart slightly larger than the wadding.

3 Cut some lace and stick this onto the back of the card as a pretty surround. Add a bow to the front and a plain piece of card to the back to write on.

4 The finished invitation.

Hearts, and fruit and leaves sprayed gold, are suitably romantic table decorations.

Party Food

Enjoy the fun of a sweethearts party with love potions and food which is supposed to have magical properties.

CHOCOLATE MOUSSE

250g (9oz) plain chocolate
3 tbsp black coffee
6 eggs

1 Break the chocolate into a bowl, add the coffee and heat over a pan of water until the chocolate is melted. Take the chocolate off the heat and leave to cool.
2 Separate the eggs and whisk the egg whites until they stand in soft peaks. Mix the egg yolks with the chocolate and fold in the egg whites. Pour the mixture into heart-shaped ramekins and leave to chill for 4 hours.

HEART-MELTING MOMENTS

175g (6oz) softened butter
50g (2oz) icing sugar
250g (9oz) self-raising flour, sifted
½ tsp salt
icing sugar to decorate

Pre-heat the oven to a temperature of 190°C (375°F, gas mark 5)
1 Mix the butter with the sugar and add the flour and the salt. Form into a dough and roll out.
2 Cut out heart-shaped biscuits either with a cutter or by eye. Bake on a greased baking tray for 8-10 minutes.
3 When cool, decorate with a light sprinkling of sifted icing sugar.

CINNAMON TOASTS

1 tsp ground
  cinnamon
3 tsp caster sugar
2 pieces of bread
  per person
heart-shaped cutter
butter

1 Mix together the cinnamon and sugar.
2 Cut the bread into heart shapes. Toast under the grill, spread with butter and sprinkle the cinnmamon and sugar mixture over the top. Eat immediately.

SAVOURY BISCUITS

small water biscuits
butter
cottage cheese
cream cheese
cheese
smoked salmon
salami
tomato
ham
cucumber

Butter the biscuits. Then cut all the other ingredients, except the cottage and cream cheese, into heart shapes and put them on the biscuits using contrasting colours and textures together. For example, cucumber and cream cheese, salmon and cottage cheese, salami and tomato.

Table Decorations

Sweetheart decorations come in all manner of sizes. To decorate the tablecloth, cover it with muslin. Cut hearts from red and pink tissue paper and sprinkle them over the table to look like rose petals, Make heart plates by cutting paper plates into heart shapes with paper doilly centres. Decorate white paper cups with red tissue hearts and stick heart-shaped swizzle sticks into drinks.

Draw hearts onto the back of red paper and arrows onto gold paper. Cut out the hearts and the arrows and also cut the arrows into three.

Stick the broken arrow onto the heart to look like it has pierced it. Puffy clouds can be sponged onto lining paper using pink and white paint and then stuck on the tablecloth. Edge the paper with twisted netting.

A Picnic Party

Picnics are fun to have anywhere and at any time. You don't have to wait for the sun to come out, you can make your own. Plan to have your picnic outside but if the weather changes for the worst, de-camp inside. You can even have indoor grass, ask your greengrocer or butcher where he got his astroturf. Or make do with a sheet spread on the carpet to make a tablecloth.

Costumes

- Turn yourself into a scarecrow with a mop head, straw or raffia for hair, stuck under an old and battered straw hat.
- Borrow old and tattered jeans, corduroys, or dungarees and wear with old misshapen sweaters or shirts with rips or buttons missing.
- To make the outfit authentic, stick a wooden spoon (stick end outwards) down your sleeves, with a few bits of straw sticking out.
- Complete the outfit with an old pair of gum boots.
- A snail wears grey tights and sweater and wears a grey globe lampshade on his back held on by grey straps. A long padded tail ending in a point is tied to the waist.
- A bee costume can be made by dressing in bright yellow tights and a yellow tee shirt painted with black stripes using a fabric pen.

Party Games

WILD WIDE GAME
This is a good game to work up a decent appetite before the picnic.

Props A long stick tied with a bright scarf showing base camp, bell.

To Play First decide on the area of play and then walk both teams around its outer rim. All together, decide where base camp is and place the stick with scarf in the middle. Team A remains at base camp while team B hides. After five minutes, team A leaves to find members of team B. One person remains at base where the team B members are sent once found. Team B can release its captured by unstaking the stick in the camp, but this can only be done by a member who has not been caught. (S)he must stealthily creep into the base camp without the team A guard seeing him/her. It is important to allow both groups to be searchers and hiders.

MUSICAL TREES
This game can become musical statues if the outside has to be abandoned.

Props Tape recorder, music tape

To Play Children dance/run to the music within the designated area of play. When the music stops, players must run to the tree nearest to them. The last child to reach the safety of a tree is out. This continues until one child is left who is declared the winner.

WHEELBARROW RACE
Remember to play this before the picnic as it can be rather strenuous.

Props Tape to act as finishing line with one end tied and the other held/tied loosely.

To Play Children are placed in pairs. One child acts as the handles of the wheelbarrow by holding the legs of his/her partner. The other child becomes the front wheel and walks along on his/her hands. Children are lined up and when they hear 'Go' they then become wheelbarrows and move as quickly as possible to the finishing line. If there are a lot of children, have two heats with the fastest two pairs from each having a final race.

Room Decorations

Crepe paper grass is made by cutting strips of green crepe paper about 20 cms (8ins) deep which are then cut into zigzags to look like long grass. On a photocopier, enlarge photographs of pets or paint your own. Stick these onto cardboard, cut around the animals and then tape a piece of card onto the back at right angles to make a stand. You can now have cats, dogs or any other pet you fancy at your party. Encourage your children to paint large fluffy rain clouds, rain and the sun, cut these out and stick them on the walls.

A sandwich invitation is made by cutting a piece of card and folding it in half. Cut a piece of wadding slightly larger than the card (once halved) and stick it to the front of the card. Cut a yellow piece of butter from some sticky-backed paper for the inside of the card. Then cut bits of green paper (lettuce), red (tomato) and white with yellow (egg) and position them inside the card so that they overlap the butter.

Making a papier-mâché cat

1 Using masking tape, stick a ball of paper onto the top of a large plastic bottle. Cover the ball and the bottle in strips of glued newspaper (see page 10).

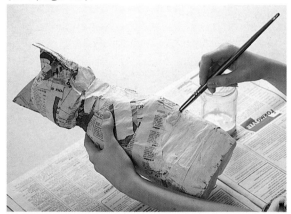

2 Cut triangular ears from card and stick onto the head (or the ball) on the top of the bottle. Paint the cat with white emulsion paint.

3 Paint the features of the cat including the face, feet, tail and markings. Give him the best seat at the picnic!

Party Food

The best sort of party is often a picnic party as children feel freer without the constraints of table manners. If the weather is bad, have your picnic inside. Serve the food from plain brown paper bags or small picnic baskets or boxes.

MULTICOLOURED SANDWICHES

white and brown cut bread
butter
fillings of different colours using any of the
**   following: chocolate spread, peanut butter,**
**   Marmite, jam, marmalade, cucumber,**
**   cheese, red and green pepper**

1 Spread the bread with butter and then any of the ingredients.
2 Layer the sandwiches white on top of brown, brown on top of white using as many different fillings as possible.
3 Cut off all the crusts using a sharp knife and make the sandwiches child bite size.

EGGY CATERPILLARS

1 cos lettuce
6 eggs, hard boiled
mayonnaise or
**   salad cream**
cocktail onions
cocktail sticks

1 Wash and separate the lettuce leaves.
2 With a fork, mash the hard boiled eggs adding enough mayonnaise or salad cream to make a thick but moist mixture. Spoon the mixture into the centres of the lettuce leaves and then fold up the leaves.
3 Put cocktail onions on the ends of two sticks and insert into the body of each caterpillar. Do not forget to remove the sticks when eating.

DAISIES

cream cheese
digestive biscuits
hard yellow or orange cheese

1 Pipe the cream cheese onto the biscuits in petal shapes to form a daisy.
2 Using a round petit-four cutter, cut circles of hard cheese to make the centres of the daisies.

SAUSAGE HEDGEHOG

cocktail sausages
cocktail sticks
half a grapefruit
olive
liquorice strips

1 To make the hedgehog's nose, attach an olive to the grapefruit using half a cocktail stick. Add liquorice eyelashes, also using pieces of cocktail stick.
2 Bake the cocktail sausages in the oven until they are cooked. When cool, spear with cocktail sticks and stick into the grapefruit.

CHEESE WORMS

225g (8oz) packet puff pastry
450g (1lb) Cheddar cheese

Pre-heat the oven to a temperature of 425°C (220°F, gas mark 7)
1 Roll out the pastry as a long strip until it is very thin.
2 Grate cheese onto the pastry, fold the pastry in half lengthwise and roll it again. Grate on more cheese, fold the pastry in half again and roll it out flat.
3 Cut the cheese pastry into long worms and bake on a greased baking sheet for 5 to 10 minutes.

Table Decorations

Fake flowers made from tissue or crepe paper and/or fabric or plastic are great decorations for an astroturf picnic table on the floor. Alternatively, make a floor covering from real leaves if it is autumn, or paper leaves decorated in reds, greens and yellows. Have a proper gingham cloth in red or blue and if you are lucky enough to own a real picnic basket use this for the centre of your festivities. Or make your own from a basket or even a cardboard box (see A Teddy Bears Picnic) and fill it with brightly coloured paper plates and mugs.

A Seaside Party

Oh I do like to be beside the seaside! What fun a party would be beside the sea, or even under the sea. Here at last is something to do with all those pebbles, shells and seaweed your children made you bring back from your last holiday. Hold the party at the real seaside or make your own with flotsam and jetsam — we show you how.

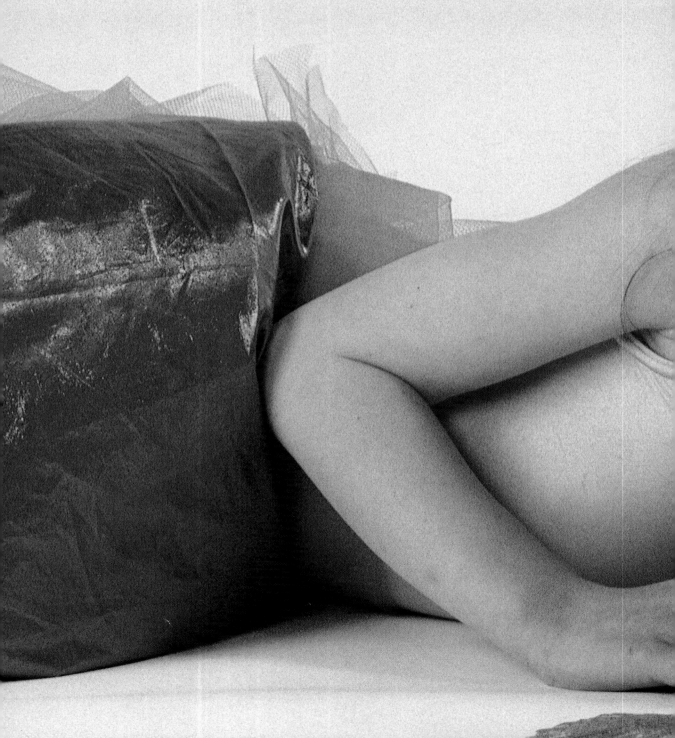

Costumes

- Make a mermaid from a plain pink swimsuit wrapped round with netting to which a padded and appliquéd fish tail is attached.
- Stick shells on lamé fabric as a headband.
- For Neptune, make a tabard (see page 11) from tissue lamé in silver, blue or green, tied with seaweed or a belt made of shells.
- Make his trident from an old fire iron or cut one from card and attach it to silver-sprayed dowelling.
- Cut fish-shaped masks from card and paint them with tropical fish colours and patterns.
- Make a fish tail by painting scales using a glitter pen on polycotton.
- Be a diver and wear a snorkel, face mask and a rubber suit or black leotard.
- Be a sand castle made from corrugated cardboard with shells and beached star fish stuck or drawn on. Hold a flag above your head.
- Mr Punch can be made by wearing an enormous papier-mâché nose (see page 10), a cap with a bell (see elf costume, page 23) and a ruff.

Making a Goldfish Bowl

1 Fill the bottom of the bowl with sugared almonds or other rock-like sweets. Cut angelica into slices and anchor this between the almonds.

2 Add real and chocolate shells to the bottom of the bowl. Add lengths of fresh dill.

3 Make three or four small, papier-mâché fish (see A Pirate party, page 91) and also add these to the bowl.

Party Games

These games can all be played on the beach, but if the party is at home they can easily be adapted for indoor/garden play.

SAND CASTLE COMPETITION

Again this can be a team game or can be played by individuals.

Props One bucket and spade per child.

To Play Children are divided into teams and told to find a large space. On the word 'Go' each team has to make as many sand castles with their buckets and spades as possible before you call,

'Stop'. The team with the largest number of complete castles wins. If you are on a pebbly beach, then each team has to make one castle but the object here is to build it as high and as stable as possible. The tallest structure wins as long as it stands until the end of the party!

KNOCK THE ROCK

This is definitely an outdoors game.

Props Stones of varying sizes.

To Play Build a mound of stones or a mound of sand

with a couple of stones on top. On top of the pile put a larger, distinctive stone which has to be knocked off. If playing this game in teams have one mound per team. Each member collects his/her ammunition (three stones) and then stands at a set distance away from the target. Team members throw stones at the top of the mound to knock off the topmost stone. The first team to successfully hit their target off its perch wins. If no one succeeds, each player collects another three stones and they all try again.

Party Food

The food of the sea is delicious, especially if it is concocted by you. As well as these exciting recipes, why not also serve crab sticks, prawns and chocolate fish, and make jellies in lobster or fish jelly moulds?

CROISSANT CRABS

small croissants
red peppers
tomato paste
cream cheese
hard cheese,
    such as Cheddar
currants

1 Cut the croissants through the middle. Cut the pepper into lengthways strips and then halve each strip across the middle.
2 Mix a little tomato paste with the cream cheese until it is a pinky colour.
3 Cut wedges of cheese 5mm deep × 2cms long × 7.5cms wide (¼in deep × ¾in long × 3ins wide). Cut a V-shape into one of the 7.5cm (3in) sides.
4 Spread the cream cheese on the croissants. Place four pepper legs out of each side of the croissant and the wedge-shaped cheese at the ends of the croissant and the large claws.
5 Put back the tops of the croissants. Use cheese paste to stick on currant eyes.

ROCK POOLS

1 packet green jelly
blue food colouring
brown food colouring
1 packet marzipan
angelica
shrimp-shaped sweets and jelly snakes

1 Mix the green jelly according to the instructions on the packet. Add some blue food colouring.
2 Add some brown food colouring to the marzipan and make rock and boulder shapes.
3 In glass serving dishes, put the boulders, followed by strips of angelica seaweed at the sides and shrimps and sea snakes. Pour the jelly on top and leave to set.

SAND CASTLE CAKES

quantity cake mix (see page 15)
paper cake cases
butter icing (see page 15)
caster sugar
cocktail sticks
pieces of coloured paper
100s and 1000s

1 Mix together the ingredients as on page 15 and bake in the paper cake cases for 15 minutes. Turn out of the cases and leave upside down. Cover the new tops and sides with butter icing and dip into caster sugar.
2 Make flags from the cocktail sticks and paper. Stick into the rock cakes. Roll the edges of the sand castles in 100s and 1000s.

Table Decorations

Fish-shaped table mats are cut from paper and decorated with paper collage fish. These and the food can then be placed on a tablecloth of blue netting — props of papier-mâché (see page 10) such as fish (see A Pirate Party, page 91), buckets and spades, pebbles, and mermaids can be maid. Or use lining paper, paint it pale blue and decorate it with a wavy sea pattern.

Shell-shaped paper plates can be made by painting paper plates pale pink and cutting them into shell shapes. Or how about using real large shells, meticulously washed of course, as plates? As a suitably fishy centrepiece for the table, either make a fish-shaped cake or fill a goldfish bowl full of pretend paper fish, pebbles and weed. The weed could be made from angelica and the pebbles sugared almonds.

A Nursery Rhyme Party

Here is a great opportunity to be your favourite nursery rhyme character be it big and bold like the bad wolf or one of the three little pigs. A girl with long blond hair will make a wonderful Goldilocks. Simple masks and props will suggest characters so you do not need to spend a vast amount of time on this party.

Costumes

- Little Red Riding Hood's dress (see picture on previous page) can simply be a pretty party dress with frills.
- Make a red cloak as described on page 11.
- Little Boy Blue (see picture on previous page) can be made from any blue costume – an old page boy's costume would be ideal, especially worn with a blue beret and carrying a horn.
- Little Miss Muffet's mobcap can be made from a 75cm (30in) circle of fabric with elastic inserted 10cms (4ins) from the outside edge to make a frill.
- To complete the outfit, carry a bowl and spoon for curds and whey and a plastic spider.
- Make the Little Pig mask as described opposite.
- Simple Simon's pie man wears a chef's apron and has a pasty under his arm.

Party Games

This theme obviously lends itself to parties for the very young. The concentration span of 2 and 3-year-olds is not very long so remember to have many more games planned than you may expect.

HERE WE GO ROUND THE MULBERRY BUSH

This is a good one to start with and can be shortened or lengthened depending on how long you wish it to last.

Props None.

To Play Children stand in a circle holding hands. Explain that they will walk round in the circle to sing the chorus 'Here we go round the mulberry bush . . .', then stop to sing a verse. Each child can choose a verse such as 'This is the way we brush our hair . . .', or you can lead all the way through.

PASS THE PARCEL

This is a popular game with which to end and can be made shorter or longer by more or less wrapping round the parcel.

Props Small gift wrapped in several layers of newspaper which can be taped or loosely tied with string. A tape recorder preferably with a nursery rhyme tape or any other music.

To Play Children sit in a circle with one child holding the parcel. When the music begins, the parcel is passed from child to child. As soon as the music stops, the player who is left holding the parcel removes a layer of newspaper as quickly as possible. (S)he continues removing layers until the music begins again. This carries on until all paper is removed and the one who rips off the last layer wins the prize. A small gift or sweet can be put in every layer so that all players have a prize at some stage during the game and this makes a pleasant ending to the party.

NURSERY RHYME CHARADES

This game is for slightly older children to play.

Props None.

To Play Everyone sits in a circle and you ask if there is any player who would like to act out a nursery rhyme. Some children find this easy while others may need you to suggest a rhyme such as 'Humpty Dumpty'. You whisper to the child what to do and in this case direct him/her to just sit on an imagined chair and fall off. This is repeated several times until one of the others guesses correctly. This child then gets his/her turn. Some suggestions are as follows: Miss Muffet who again sits on an imaginary chair pretending to eat from a bowl. When the spider comes she screams and runs away. Jack Horner is straightforward – Jack sits in the corner with his pie. He puts his thumb in the pretend pie, pulls it out looking smug and smiles. Prizes can be awarded for each successful act.

RING-A-RING O' ROSES

This is a good game to follow the first as the children are still standing in a circle.

Props None.

To Play All children join hands in a circle and walk round while singing the song 'Ring-a-ring o' roses'. If you want to vary the traditional 'All fall down' part of the song and make it into a game then the last child to fall down can be out. This continues until only one child is left who is the winner.

Making a Pig Mask

1 Hold a paper plate up to your face and mark the position of your eyes, nose and mouth with a pencil. Cut out the eye holes. Attach a length of black elastic.

2 To make a nose, squash a small fromage frais carton and stick it on the plate. Paint the plate and the nose pink and add a pink mouth with a felt pen.

3 Cut out pink felt ears and attach to the back of the mask.

4 The completed mask.

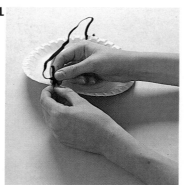

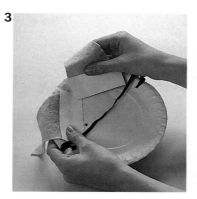
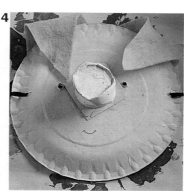

Table Decorations

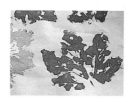

A leaf print tablecloth requires a collection of well-shaped leaves with prominent veins. Cut a piece of lining paper large enough for your table. Pour green, yellow, and brown poster paints into separate saucers. Brush paint onto the underside of each leaf and place it paint side down onto the paper. Press hard and lift the leaf. Continue until the table is covered in leaves of different colours. Cut-out leaf prints make good wall decorations.

A gingerbread house as a table centre would be perfect. Make the gingerbread from 700g (1½lb) plain flour, 2tsp baking soda, 2tsp salt, 1tsp cloves, nutmeg, 2tsp ginger, 2tsp cinnamon, 450g (1lb) vegetable shortening, 450g (1lb) sugar, 350g (12oz) black treacle, 4 eggs (beaten). Mix all the ingredients in a food mixer. Divide the mixture into six, and roll out two sides, a front and a back and two roofs.

Bake on a greased baking tray in a pre-heated oven at a temperature of 180°C (350°F, gas mark 4) for 15-20 minutes. Use glacé icing (see page 15) to stick the house together and then decorate with biscuits, sweets and chocolates.

Party Food

Food often appears in nursery rhymes, from the big bad wolf who dearly wished to eat three little pigs to Simple Simon who met a pie man on the way to the fair. So why not eat some of this food at your nursery rhyme party?

QUEEN OF HEARTS JAM TARTS

200g (7oz) shortcrust pastry (see page 15)
red jam

Pre-heat the oven to a temperature of 200°C (400°F, gas mark 6)
1 Roll out the pastry and cut with circular cutters. Place on a greased indented baking tray and prick the bottom of each small pastry case. Fill each one with 1 tsp of jam and decorate with heart-shaped pieces of pastry.
2 Bake for 10-12 minutes, until the pastry is golden brown.

SIMPLE SIMON'S PIE MAN PIES

200g (7oz) shortcrust pastry (see page 15)
175g (6oz) chuck steak
110g (4oz) potato, peeled
1 small onion, peeled
pepper and salt
1 tbsp water
beaten egg or milk

Pre-heat the oven to a temperature of 200°C (400°F, gas mark 6)
1 Divide the pastry into four and roll out each piece in a circle.
2 Cut the meat into narrow strips, dice the potato and chop the onion. Mix the filling with seasoning and water. Pile quarter of the mixture onto each of the pastry circles. Damp the edge of the circle and fold in half, enclosing the filling. Press the edges together firmly. Brush the top with beaten egg or milk.
3 Bake on a greased baking tray for 20 minutes at 200°C (400°F, gas mark 6) and then turn the oven down to 170°C (325°F, gas mark 3) for a further 30 minutes.

HOT CROSS BUNS

250g (9oz) strong
   plain flour
25g (1oz) yeast
50g (2oz) sugar
½ tsp salt
110g (4oz) margarine
150ml (¼pt) milk
1 egg
½ level tsp mixed spice
25g (1oz) currants or sultanas

Pre-heat the oven to a temperature of 200°C (400°F, gas mark 6)
1 Make the dough mixing together the flour, yeast, 25g (1oz) of sugar, salt, 25g (1oz) margarine and milk. Knead well and leave to rise in a warm place.
2 After the first rising, add the rest of the ingredients and shape the mixture into 8-10 balls, depending on the size required. Mark a cross in the top of each with a knife. Leave to rise again and then bake on a greased baking tray for 20-25 minutes, until cooked.

LITTLE MISS MUFFET SPIDER WEB CAKES

quantity cake mix
   (see page 15)
1 tbsp cocoa powder
paper cake cases
paper, pencil and
   scissors
icing sugar

Pre-heat the oven to a temperature of 200°C (400°F, gas mark 6)
1 Mix together the ingredients as on page 15 but add the cocoa powder to the mixture. Bake in the paper cake cases for 15 minutes and leave the cakes to cool.
2 Cut a spider's web template from the paper and lay on each cake. Sprinkle icing sugar through the template to produce a spider's web pattern.

A Teddy Bears' Picnic

If you go down to the woods today you're sure of a big surprise. Adults and children alike love teddy bears and their picnics. If the weather is inclement, make a picnic and have it indoors at home. See if you can borrow some astroturf from your local butcher, or use a green sheet or even a picnic rug. Make sure to take your best beloved bear with you.

Costumes

- Make a teddy hood made from fake fur using the pattern featured on page 14.
- Make the body of the teddy using the all-in-one pattern featured on pages 12-13.
- For a simpler costume, attach round ears made from fake fur lined in pink felt to a headband and blacken your nose.
- Wear brown woollen mittens for paws
- A teddy mask is made from card covered in felt.
- For a fat teddy tummy, wear a brown sweater and tights with a small cushion stuffed inside the sweater.
- Rupert Bear's scarf is made from a plain yellow scarf decorated with a black fabric-paint grid.

Room Decorations

Brightly coloured teddy bears greatly enliven the party room. Draw teddy outlines onto coloured paper and cut them out. Add cheerful, smiling faces with black felt pen and then stick them onto the walls.

Opposite: table decorations are really simple to make for a teddy bear's picnic. Instructions are provided here for picnic baskets (see opposite), teddy place names and bear plates (see overleaf).

Party Games

Every child should arrive at the party with a teddy bear though do make sure you have some spares in case some bears do not arrive for one reason or another!

MUSICAL TEDDY BUMPS

An old favourite with a teddy bear theme.

Props One bear for each child, tape recorder, tape, (if possible with 'Teddy Bears' Picnic' included).

To Play Bears are scattered on the ground and children dance round to the music. When the music stops, each child picks up a bear as quickly as possible and sits down with it — the bear does not have to be their own. The last child to sit down with a bear is out. This continues until there is only one player left and (s)he is declared the winner.

TEDDY CAN WE COME FOR TEA?

This is a game for younger children and one in which the teddies can be involved.

Props None, but it would be fun if all children had a teddy to hold as well as you as caller.

To Play Children all stand facing you holding their teddies. They all shout 'Mr Teddy can we come for tea?' You respond by saying 'No, you cannot unless you have a teddy and a pair of blue shoes'. Those children with blue shoes can then cross over to where you are standing and sit ready for their tea. Each time the remaining children ask the questions you reply with 'No, you cannot come unless you have a teddy and . . .'. You must think of some item or colour of clothing to complete the sentence. This continues until all the children are sitting ready for their teddy bears' picnic.

TEDDY SAYS

This is a variation on the game 'Simon Says' which keeps younger children amused for quite a while.

Props None.

To Play Children find a space in which to stand and you stand in front facing them. You may like to hold the teddy again just for fun. When you say 'Teddy says clap your hands', all children clap their hands and continue to do so until you give the next direction such as 'Teddy says jump up and down' or 'Teddy says stand on one foot'. The children follow all orders unless you say for example 'Tap your head'. They should not do this because Teddy has not said to do it. Any child who accidentally does this is out. This continues until only one child is left.

The Teddy Bears' Picnic Baskets

1 Use a shoe box for each picnic basket. Spread wall-paper paste onto plenty of pieces of kitchen paper and roll them into strips. Stick them to the box in a criss-cross fashion.

2 Paint each box either brown or yellow ochre.

3 Attach cardboard handles to the sides of the box or tape the lid to the box bottom to look like a proper basket.

Party Food

As any one who has read Winnie the Pooh or Paddington Bear will know, teddies love food and especially picnics. The odd honey or marmalade sandwich goes down particularly well.

BEAR SANDWICHES

1 loaf of bread, brown or white
butter
honey
marmalade
teddy bear cutter

Make the sandwiches filling them with butter and honey or marmalade. Cover in cling film and put in the fridge for an hour. Remove the crusts and stamp out the bear shapes.

TEDDY CAKES

quantity cake mix (see page 15)
paper cake cases
glacé icing (see page 15)
semi-circular glacé orange slices
chocolate beans

Pre-heat the oven to a temperature of 200°C (400°F, gas mark 6)
Mix together the ingredients as on page 15 and bake in the paper cake cases for 15 minutes. When cool, draw on teddy faces with the glacé icing. Stick on glacé orange ears and chocolate bean eyes.

TEDDY BEAR SHORTBREAD

110g (4oz) butter
110g (4oz) flour
50g (2oz) cornflour
50g (2oz) caster sugar
pinch salt
teddy bear cutter
packet of small sweets
short lengths of ribbon

Pre-heat the oven to a temperature of 170°C (325°F, gas mark 3).
1 Rub the butter into the dry ingredients to form a dough the consistency of shortcrust pastry. Roll out on a floured board and cut into teddy bear shapes.
2 Decorate with sweets for eyes and bake in the oven on a greased baking sheet for 15 minutes.
3 When cool, tie a ribbon round each bear's neck.

TEDDY JELLIES

1 packet orange jelly
1 tin satsumas
teddy-shaped jelly moulds

Make the jelly according to the packet, leave to cool and then add the satsumas to the mixture. Pour the jelly in to the moulds and put in the fridge to set. Empty out the moulds before serving.

Table Decorations

Teddy place names are made by drawing teddies with short fat legs which are close together onto stiff paper or thin card. Colour the bear and add his features. Don't forget to write on the name of the guest. Punch a hole in the teddy's ear and then add some ribbon to hang him by.

Bear plates which are china plates decorated to look like bear faces make great going home presents.
Buy seconds of white china and draw bear face outlines with a Chinagraph pencil onto each one. Then, using ceramic paint, paint in the teddy face. Bake the plate in the oven according to the manufacturer's instructions. If you are not good at painting, decorate the plate with bear paw prints.

A Jungle Party

Here is a wild party set in the jungle. Decorate the room with plenty of green crepe paper creepers, and large tissue paper butterflies and flowers to give an authentic atmosphere. Jungle costumes can be made from animal print fabrics worn over swim wear with flower garlands. Make trees from cardboard tubes with large green cartridge paper leaves.

Costumes

- Make tiger and leopard print costumes using the all-in-one pattern on page 12 and the hood pattern featured on page 14.
- A monkey tail is easily made from fake fur and fabric and then stitched onto a leotard.
- Colour the child's body with brown face paints.

- For a parrot costume — wear brightly coloured tights and tee shirt.
- Make paper wings and paint bright colours and make a hood as for the Easter chick on page 14, but with a longer bent beak.
- For a butterfly costume — wear a black leotard and tights.
- Make wings from a sheet of fabric decorated with fabric paint or appliqué. Attach onto a leotard at the wrists, shoulders and tack down the centre back.

Room Decorations

Paint **creepers** onto a backdrop and then stick this onto the wall. Also, for a truly jungle effect, make creepers by twisting crepe paper to make ropes and sticking on leaves, made as for the table decorations, paper flowers and butterflies using a glue stick. Fasten them to the ceiling and twist overhead and between the trees you make (see step-by-step sequence below). Ensure they are out of children's range. Attempted swings could result in accidents.

Party Games

The whole party can be organized using a story which unfolds as time passes.

ANIMAL SEARCH
The children are exploring the jungle and decide to see how many different species of animal they can find.

Props Six or more animals cut out of plain coloured paper (you will need as many of each animal as there are guests). These should be hidden around the house before children arrive.

To Play Every child has to collect one of each animal or one type of animal.

WHAT A SMELL!
The children are desperate for something to eat but have to check that they know what it is before tasting.

Props Ten numbered yogurt/ mousse cartons each containing a different substance such as chocolate powder, salt, washing powder, flour, cinnamon, paper and pencils.

To Play Each pot is placed on a surface, preferably in the kitchen. Every child makes his/her way round to each one trying to identify the substance in each by smelling the contents. They write their answers on the paper which is then marked by another guest. The person with the most correct guesses wins.

SHIPWRECK
The children continue to explore and suddenly find sea as far as the eye can see. On the horizon they espy a shipwreck.

Props None.

To Play You are the captain of the ship and call the orders to which the 'sailors' (children) respond. Run through all the commands before you start. These are: 'Starboard' — run to the right-hand-side of the ship, 'Port' — run to the left-hand-side of the ship, 'Bow' — run to the front of the ship, 'Stern' — run to the back, 'Climb the rigging' — children climb on the spot lifting their arms as well as their legs, 'Captain's coming' — stand to attention, 'Sharks' — everyone must stand dead still, 'Man overboard' — lie on tummies and make swimming actions. The last child to respond or to reach the side of the ship is out each time and this continues until only one person is left.

Jungle Trees

1 Cut a length of crepe paper into a 10-cm (4-in) width and cut Vs at regular intervals.

2 Using paper glue, stick the crepe paper to the tube unwinding as you go.

3 Make large green leaves from cartridge paper. Stick wire to the back, bend them, attach into top of tree trunk.

Party Food

The sounds, smells and tastes of the jungle are fresh and exotic, sometimes spicy, with fruit salads and very healthy party food. Serve bunches of fruit in season, especially bananas.

SATAY WITH PEANUT SAUCE

350g (12oz) pork fillet
cocktail sticks
1 tsp chilli powder
1 onion
1 clove garlic
1 tsp sunflower oil
2 tbsp lemon juice
5 tbsp crunchy peanut butter
1 tsp salt
1 tsp cumin powder
1 tsp coriander

1 Cut the pork into small pieces and thread three of four pieces on a cocktail stick. Cook under a pre-heated grill turning the skewers over occasionally until the meat is cooked.
2 To make the sauce, blend the chilli powder with some water to make a paste. Dice the onion, and crush the garlic. Heat the oil and add the onion, garlic, and chilli paste and fry gently to soften the onion. Add the remaining ingredients, stir well. Use as a dip with the pork.

Table Decorations

Papier-mâché fruit is made from balls of newspaper fixed into shape with masking tape and covered with strips of glued paper (see page 10). Apply three or four layers, allowing each layer to dry before pasting on the next one. Add cardboard stalks and leaves if desired. Paint the fruit with poster paints. Try making bananas, oranges, apples, pineapples and grapefruit in this way.

Palm leaf-shaped table mats are a fun way to set the scene at the tea table. Cut large pieces of crepe paper in a rough leaf shape as for the palm tree on the previous page. Do not add the wire strip down the back. Add a lighter green central vein made from light green crepe paper. For tableware, wrap paper cups in smaller green leaves of the same pattern.

ANIMAL PASTA WITH BACON

110g (4oz) streaky bacon
1 tbsp oil
50g (2oz) Parmesan cheese
3 eggs
150ml (¼pt) single cream
275g (10oz) animal pasta, cooked

De-rind the bacon and cut into small pieces. Heat the oil in a pan and add the bacon. Mix the cheese, eggs and cream together. Turn the bacon to medium heat and add the creamy mixture. Add the animal pasta. Serve at once.

FRESH JUNGLE FRUIT SALAD

fresh fruit in season, including:
apples
oranges
satsumas
bananas
kiwi
strawberries
pineapple
grapes
apple juice
coconut shell

Peel, de-pip and pith the citrus fruits. Peel and chop the other fruits and put everything into the coconut shell with the fruit juice.

TOFFEE APPLES

8 apples
8 wooden skewers
150ml (¼pt) water
350g (12oz) granulated
   sugar
175g (6oz) golden syrup
1 tsp vanilla essence
red food colouring

1 Wash and dry the apples and push skewers through the stalk end.
2 Put the other ingredients in a saucepan, and stir slowly until the sugar dissolves. Bring to the boil, cover and cook for 2 minutes. Uncover and continue to boil for a further 7-8 minutes. Colour the toffee red with a few drops of colouring.
3 Swirl the apples in the mixture, stand on a buttered dish and leave in a cool place until set.

Halloween Party

Ghosts, ghouls and things that go bump in the night all make for very exciting parties. Costumes are easy too — try creating a mummy made from loo paper, a ghost from a sheet and a witch's hat from a black card cone. Props can be constructed from simple cut outs of bats, pumpkins and black cats.

Costumes

- Make a ghost from an old sheet with two eyes holes cut out and rimmed in black paint.
- A skeleton can be made using a black tee shirt and tights with bones made of crepe paper or vylene sewn or stuck on.
- Make an Egyptian mummy by wrapping loo paper round and round a child until only the eyes show.
- For a witch (see photograph on previous page), make a hat as described opposite.
- Make a cloak as described below and appliqué it with stars and moons in metallic lamé.
- A severed hand can be made from an old rubber glove with bits of rice crispies (warts) and hair stuck on. Paint the whole thing green – it is truly revolting.
- Be a cobweb by wearing shirring elastic over a pink leotard and tights (see photograph on previous page) and add a plastic spider for good measure.

Making a Witch's Cloak

1 More detailed instructions are provided on page 11. Fold a 135cm (54in) square of black fabric into quarters. Mark a curve at the folded corner for the neck and a curve on the outer edge for the hem. Cut the hem and neck.

2 For the collar, cut a length of fabric to fit the neckline. Finish off the edges and sew onto the cloak. Attach a red ribbon tie. Neaten the hem with a running stitch.

3 Cut out tissue lamé stars and moons and appliqué these all over the cloak.

Party Games

MASKS

It would be a good idea to have the children making masks when they arrive. These could then be worn throughout the party.

Props Plain brown paper bags/paper plates (black are relatively easy to find and would be most appropriate), empty yogurt pots containing glue, lolly sticks with which to use the glue, milk bottle tops, lengths of wool in various colours, thick wax crayons, scissors, string, coloured straws, silver/gold stars, silver/gold felt tips.

To Play Each child selects a bag or plate. Help younger children to place and cut holes for eyes. Decorate the mask in any way desired using the materials provided. Hair can be added by using lengths of wool which can be glued to the bag or plate above the eyes and down the sides.

APPLES ON THE LINE

This game is great and causes much laughter.

Props String from which to hang the apples (it needs to be attached securely at both ends). Apples which have a length of string threaded through the middle. This is achieved most easily by using a skewer to bore a hole through the middle of a soft apple. Thread the string through and knot it at the lower end. Tie the stringed apples at different intervals along the string.

To Play Loosely tie the children's hands behind their back. Let each child select an apple hanging from the line which they then try to bite. This always looks a lot easier that it is! Once a player has managed to take a bite or two untie the apple which can then be finished. Replace this apple by another if there are more children to play. For younger children, use quarters or halves of the fruit which makes it easier to bite.

FEELY CAULDRON

This is a variation on an old tried and tested game – the 'Feely Bag'.

Props Pencils, paper, large metal casserole/washing up bowl which will act as the caudron, lid/cover to hide contents in vessel. Suggestions for contents – plastic/rubber spider, moss (from the garden/local florist), furry mouse/small animal, wooden spoon, pumice stone, sponge, prune/sultanas, tea bag.

To Play Place about ten objects in the cauldron (put five in two containers if younger children) and cover it up. Turn all the lights off so as to make it as near to pitch dark as possible. Each child then has a chance to feel the contents and then must wait until the lights go up before writing down as many as they recognise. If there is time, children may have another chance to feel. The child who guesses the most number of objects correctly, wins.

Room Decorations

Witches' hats are fun to make. Draw around a large dinner plate onto black card. Cut out the circle and then cut it in half – each half makes one hat. Take one half and glue together the two straight edges to make a cone. For the brim, measure the circumference of the hat and cut another circle with a circumference 5cms (2ins) wider. Draw a circle 7.5cms (3ins) in from the edge and cut on this line. Discard the centre circle. At even intervals, cut lines to a depth of 2.5cms (1in) around the brim. Bend back at right angles to the brim and stick onto the inside of the hat. Stick gold stars and moons over the hat.

Paper streamers for a halloween party require a length of black crepe paper measuring 10cms (4ins) wide. Fold the strip into a concertina so that each fold is about 7.5cms (3ins) wide. Draw a bat on the front of the concertina and then cut it out being careful not to cut down the sides of the wings as this is where they will join together. Open out the streamer. Do the same on orange crepe paper with a pumpkin design.

Party Food

The witching hour: the time when we like to have fun and frighten ourselves. Even the food can be ghoulish with a dish of fingers (sausages) and eyeballs (grapes), and a man's intestines (spaghetti).

MARSHMALLOW SPIDERS

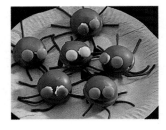

glacé icing
(see page 15)
chocolate beans
1 packet long
liquorice strips
1 packet chocolate
marshmallow
biscuits

Use the glacé icing to glue the eyes and liquorice legs to the marshmallow spider bodies.

MARZIPAN FROGS

1 packet marzipan
green and brown food colouring

Mix most of the marzipan with a few drops of green food colouring. Make smaller amounts of light green and brown marzipan. Mould the dark green marzipan into frog shapes and add other colours for eyes and patterns.

SEVERED HAND SANDWICHES

loaf of bread, white or brown
butter
tomato ketchup
sliced ham (one piece per person)

1 Press your hand into one piece of bread to make an impression then cut round the impression. Repeat with another slice. Butter the two pieces.
2 Rip a piece of ham so that the edges are tattered and place it on one piece of bread. Spread ketchup near the edges of the ham to look like blood. Put the top on the sandwich.

COCONUT GHOSTS

2 egg whites
110g (4oz) caster sugar
110g (4oz) desiccated coconut
rice paper
chocolate drops
glacé icing (see page 15)

Pre-heat the oven to a temperature of 150°C (200°F, gas mark 2).
1 Whisk the egg whites until stiff. Fold in the sugar and coconut. Put rice paper on a baking tray and spoon on the mixture in cone shapes. Cook for 40 minutes until crisp but not brown on the outside and soft in the centre.
2 Stick on the chocolate drops as eyes using the glacé icing.

Table Decorations

Pumpkin plates can be made from white cardboard plates painted orange or covered in orange crepe paper.
For each plate, cut two triangles for eyes, a diamond-shaped nose and a set of zigzag teeth from black card and stick these onto the plate. Add a black stalk, sticking it out of the top of the plate. Decorate cups with black flying bats. Also make miniature pumpkin faces and stick them on cocktail sticks to adorn sandwiches.

An Outer Space Party

From the man in the moon to the exploration of space, the idea of rockets, stars and galaxies always grabs the imagination of children. Bicycle or crash helmets make convincing space helmets, wellies can be painted silver and tin foil over cardboard makes easy costumes. Props can be made by recycling tin foil dishes and milk bottle tops.

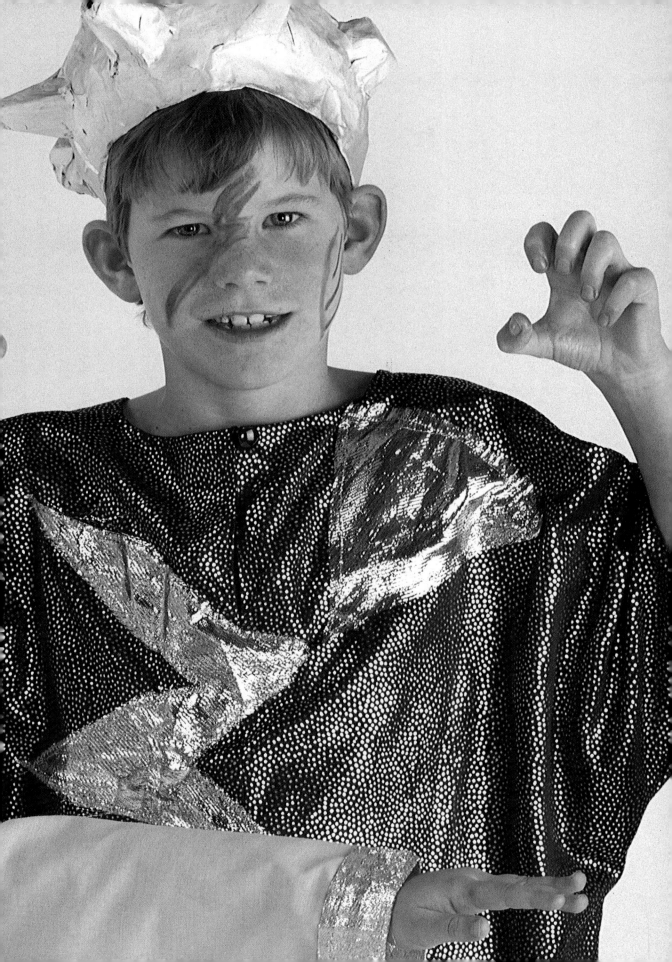

Costumes

- For a space man (see photograph on previous page), wear a tabard (see page 11) in grey or metallic fabric over white or silver tights and tee shirt.
- Make a backpack from a cardboard box covered in silver foil attached with elastic shoulder straps.
- Spray wellies silver.
- Wear a motorbike helmet.
- Make a robot costume from cardboard covered in old screws, washers, milk bottle tops and parts of egg boxes.
- For the man in the moon, cut out a cardboard crescent moon and paint it silver. Attach it with straps and wear grey tights and a sweater beneath.
- A star costume can be made from a star-shaped piece of cardboard sprayed with silver and a tinsel edging attached.
- For a star headdress, use a headband with wire attached which has been bent into a star shape and wrapped in tinsel.
- An alien (see photograph on previous page) can be made by covering a balloon in papier-mâché, sticking on bits of egg box and cutting out a space for the face. Spray the whole thing silver.

Room Decorations

Paper lampshades, either bought as grey or pale blue or yellow, make excellent outer space room decorations. Use a glue stick and glitter or a glitter glue stick to decorate patches of the lamp. Stick on silver stars and then thread more stars onto thin silver wire and tie this to the top of the lampshade. Let it twist round the lampshade, standing slightly away from it, and then attach it to the bottom.

A robot made from cardboard boxes is really effective (above and left). Use a large box for the body and then stick on a smaller one for the head and even smaller ones for the arms, legs and feet – shoe boxes are ideal for this. Decorate the whole by either spraying it with silver or covering it with tin foil and sticking on old tin cans, bits of tubing, cogs, wheels or light bulbs (see right).

Party Games

The games suggested here are for older children, aged seven or eight and above.

PLANET PLODDING

This is a boisterous and excellent game with which to begin.

Props Balloons (enough for at least two for each child), string.

To Play Tie a 60 cm (2ft) piece of string to each balloon. When children arrive they are given two balloons and asked to attach one each to their ankles. They can practise walking about while guests arrive but must be careful not to burst either balloon. The idea of this game is to walk around testing the planet's surface but while doing this burst balloons belonging to other space explorers by treading/jumping on them. Once both balloons are burst the child is out and the winner is the last one who has one or two balloons left.

NOISES FROM OUTER SPACE

This is rather a tame game to follow the Planet Plodding.

Props Pencils, paper, ten objects with which to make a sound such as newspaper, velcro, keys, opening a can, shaking a bag with milk bottle tops, recorder, sandpaper, shutting a book, closing a spectacle case, striking a match, cutting a piece of paper, etc.

To Play Each child has a piece of paper and pencil. You hide behind a sofa with the props. You say, 'Sound number one' and proceed to make the noise. Allow enough time for each child to write down what they think it might be and then go on to sound number two and so on. At the end, pass the papers to the right and go through each sound with them. The winner is the one with the most correct answers. This game can also be played in teams.

SPACE TREASURES

This game is useful as it can easily be extended or shortened and can be played in one room or the whole house.

Props Tape recorder, music tape, enough of the following for at least one each per child – buttons, beans, rice, pencils, spoons, playing cards, tissues, smarties, etc., one container per child for treasure.

To Play Place all items to be found in various parts of the room/house – some hidden and some obvious. All players are given a container each in which to collect their treasures. Music is then played while the children dance but when it stops you call, 'Search for beans'. Everyone then has to find one or more beans, continuing to look until the music begins again. When the music stops the next time you call 'Search for rice' and off the children go again looking for rice until they hear the music. You repeat this for as many times as you wish. The child with the highest number of individual items at the end, wins.

Table Decorations

Starry or rocket glasses are a must for a party such as this. First, stick the edge of each glass under a tap and dip them into a bowl of sugar to make a sparkly rim. Then stick stars cut out from silver foil all over the glasses. Make plates from foil plates cut into star shapes. Make rocket feet from silver card, and then stick onto the bottom of the glass. The tablecloth can be blue, with a Milky Way made from silver glitter and sequins, and planets and shooting stars stencilled on top.

Party Food

You can have great fun with this party food. It is easy to make sputniks, robots and flying saucer burgers — just make sure your guests don't try flying them.

CHOCOLATE ROBOTS

miniature chocolate
   swiss rolls
small sweets
silver balls
chocolate
   matchsticks

Lie the swiss rolls flat and decorate so they look just like robots.

POTATO METEORITES

1 baked potato per person, wrapped in foil
peppers
carrots
sweet corn
cucumber

Split open the potatoes, cut the ingredients in to slivers. Fill the potatoes and stick them through the foil to add to the meteorite effect.

SPUTNIK

half a grapefruit
cocktail sticks
cheese, cut into chunks
pineapple chunks
glacé cherries
cucumber, cut into chunks

Lay the grapefruit on a plate with its rounded end up. Pierce each piece of food with a cocktail stick and stick it into the grapefruit to form a sputnik.

FLYING SAUCER BURGERS

burgers (bought or made from mince meat)
cheese squares
burger buns, smaller in size than the burgers
cocktail onions
cocktail sticks

1 Cook the burgers under the grill. Cut the cheese into circles with a pastry cutter and place on top of the burger.
2 Place the burgers and cheese in the flying saucer buns and spike the top with cocktail onions on cocktail sticks. (Remember to remove them before eating.)

Decorating a Sky-at-night Tablecloth

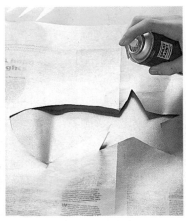

1 Draw and cut out a shooting star stencil from newspaper.

2 Cover your work surface with paper to prevent it from being covered with paint. Hold the stencil down firmly and spray silver paint through the stencil.

3 Spray a gold aura over silver planets. Lift the stencil off vertically.

Cowboys and Indians

This is a great party for boys and girls as there are so many roles they can play: cowboys, Indian chiefs, braves or squaws, saloon girls or even a horse. Paint cacti on a backdrop and decorate old school shirts with fringing or frogging. Bandannas round the neck and sheriff stars all help with the authenticity of this party.

Costumes

- A chief's headdress can be made from feathers from a duster sewn onto brown fabric as described to the right.
- Make a squaw's dress as described below.
- Use face paints to decorate the squaws' and braves' faces.
- For a cowboy shirt, use an old school shirt and add fringing.
- Jeans too can be decorated with fringing down the sides.
- Wear an old denim jacket or a waistcoat.
- Cowboy hats can be cheaply bought from a toy shop or bend an old fedora trilby into shape.
- Make a poncho from an old blanket or wrap.
- For a sheriff's badge, cut out a cardboard star and paint it silver. Stick a pin on the back to attach.

A squaw dress (above) is made by making a brown tabard (see page 11) from cotton fabric, suedette or real suede. Sew up the sides but leave room for the arms. Cut from the bottom of the skirt up 20cms (8ins) at 2.5cm (1in) intervals to make fringing. Cut a slit of 15cms (6ins) in the front of the neck. Cut eye holes and thread them with a brown lace. Decorate the neckline with beads or feathers. Add bunches of coloured feathers cut from a feather duster and sew all over the costume. Add coloured buttons to the place where you have sewn on the feathers.

Indian Chief Headdress

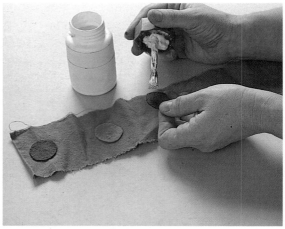

1 Cut a piece of brown fabric long enough to go round the forehead and come down the sides of the body. Taper the ends. Stick on brightly coloured circles of felt.

2 Remove feathers from brightly coloured feather dusters.

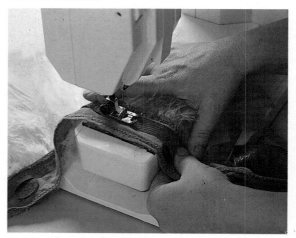

3 Machine the feathers in place using a zigzag stitch.

Party Games

The theme of this party conjures up all sorts of imaginative, noisy games which would be best played in a large space but can also be accommodated inside.

DON'T GET CAUGHT WITH THE BRIDLE

Props Cushion, rope for a bridle, tape recorder, tape with music.

To Play Make a bridle by making two circles of rope and tying them together with a length of 15cms (6ins) long. Sit the children in a circle and start the music. The bridle must be passed around until the music stops. The child with the bridle must put their arms through the two circles of rope with the length between over their shoulders and get down on all fours. (S)he then chooses another child to have a ride on his/her back. The horse then moves round the outside of the circle with its rider making appropriate noises and moving in the most horselike fashion possible. Once round the circle play resumes. A prize can be given for the couple who imitate a horse and rider the best.

HORSE SHOES

A very popular outdoor game still played in the American outback. An indoor adaptation is given here.

Props Two sticks to be used as stakes, two lassoos made from rope or a plastic washing line, a length of rope to act as a marker. Traditionally, this game is played with two metal stakes and four horse shoes which, if available, would be ideal.

To Play Place the stakes in the ground and position the length of rope some distance away from the stakes behind which the team must stand to take aim. Each child in turn is given three opportunities to try to lassoo the stake by throwing the rope while holding onto the other end. The team with the highest number of successful attempts wins. If horse shoes are available, each child throws two horse shoes at the stake trying to get the shoe round the stake.

If the game is to be played inside, use ping pong balls and buckets. Mark the floor with the rope and each child stands behind the rope before trying to throw a ping pong ball into the bucket.

WHATEVER WILL I FIND

Guests will be launched into this game as soon as their coats are taken off and it will keep them occupied for some time.

Props Several balls of string, small prizes (enough for each player).

To Play Tie one end of a piece of string to the prize. Put the prize somewhere in the house and feed the string in and out of bannisters, chair legs, round corners, under sofas, etc., arriving near the front door. With fresh pieces of string, repeat the exercise so that each child will have an end of string presented to him/her

on arrival. Each participant then has to follow their string, unravelling it as they go until they find the prize at the end. When setting this game out try not to cross other pieces of string if the children are young. If you have older players they must be warned not to disturb a neighbouring string when going over or under it.

COWBOYS AND INDIANS

Encourage children to come to the party as cowboys or indians which will always help to add to imaginative play.

Props Rope or thick string, enough cowboy hats or similar for half the number of children (they will be representing the cowboys).

To Play Divide the children into two teams 'Cowboys' and 'Indians'. One team member stands separately while the rest get into pairs and stand/sit back to back. You tie each pair up with string, tying several knots, and when you shout 'Go' the spare team member has to undo all the cowboys or all the Indians in his/her team. The first team to have all its members free wins. If there is an extra child play the game again. If this game is played outside, children could be tied to trees or garden furniture instead of each other. Once free, team members can make appropriate noises such as whooping or warbling to encourage the speed of their rescuer.

Room Decorations

For a totem pole collect lots of boxes of different sizes. Stick them together as above. For the face, use pieces of egg box for the eyes and a folded piece of cardboard for the nose. Then paint the whole thing with white emulsion paint to give a base coat. When the emulsion is dry, draw patterns (such as those featured above) onto the totem pole. Colour them with water or poster colour paints.

Party Food

Cowboy and Indian food is not the most sophisticated but it is filling, basic, and the sort of food children love. If possible, eat your feast round a camp fire, real or pretend.

BRANDED POTATOES

1 potato per person
sweetcorn
grated cheese

Pre-heat the oven to a temperature of 200°C (400°F, gas mark 6)
Clean the potatoes and then with a knife cut the initials of each child into the sides to look like cattle branding. Bake the potatoes, cut side up, until ready. Serve with sweetcorn and grated cheese.

BAKED BEANS AND RUSTLERS RIBS

1 can baked beans
3 spare ribs per person
2 tsp soy sauce
2 tsp Worcestershire sauce
4 tbsp tomato ketchup
2 tbsp marmalade
1 tsp mustard
2 tsp brown sugar

Pre-heat the oven to a temperature of 200°C (400°F, gas mark 6)
Apart from the beans and ribs, mix together all the other ingredients. Coat each rib with the sauce and leave to marinade in an ovenproof dish for 2-3 hours. Serve with the baked beans.

HOMEMADE BURGERS

450g (1lb) minced beef
1 small onion
salt and pepper
pinch of mixed herbs
1 egg
burger buns

1 Put the mince in a bowl. Peel and finely chop the onion, and add to the mince with the salt, pepper and herbs. Add the egg and mix well.
2 Divide the mixture into eight portions and roll into balls and then flatten them with your hands into burgers. Grill for 8-10 minutes. Serve with burger buns.

GARLIC BREAD

butter
French stick
clove of garlic
foil

Pre-heat the oven to a temperature of 200°C (400°F, gas mark 6)
1 Cut the bread into 2.5cm (1in) slices about two-thirds of the way through the loaf. Soften the butter with a knife.
2 Put the garlic in a garlic press and press over the butter. Mix the garlic with the butter and then spread garlic butter on each slice of the French loaf. Wrap in foil and bake in the oven for 20 minutes.

A Pirate Party

A pirate party is sure to be filled with action and surprises. With a few simple props and a little preparation, your home can be transformed into a smuggler's cove or a bucaneer's galleon — and it is sure to be an honest seafarer's worst nightmare!

Costumes

- Neckerchiefs or bandanas tied around the neck or head.
- Black eye patch made from felt or card.
- Swords made from card covered in foam wrapped in silver coloured tape. Daggers and cutlasses can be made from card and covered in tin foil.
- Moustaches painted on with a black or brown eyebrow pencil.
- Card hats with white felt skull and crossbones added.
- Striped tee shirts.

Table Decorations

Table mats can look like treasure maps. Draw a map onto a sheet of paper, preferably using a dip pen and a bottle of ink so that you can make some splodges for authenticity. Age the map by rubbing a cold wet tea bag over it. When dry, burn the edges very carefully over a gas hob. To decorate cups and plates cut out skull and crossbones in black. Stick onto white paper cups and plates.

Party Games

MUSICAL ISLANDS

This is a great game for a pirate party. It is also a game where you can involve your own children in the prop making.

Props Islands drawn on paper (you will need as many islands as there are guests), a tape recorder and a music tape (sea shanties are a good idea).

To Play Place the islands on the sea (the floor) and when the music plays the children must move around the water. As soon as the music stops, they have to run to an island. Next time the music plays, remove an island as the children are moving round. The child who doesn't land on an island when the music stops is out. Continue in this way until there are only two children left in the game and one island. The child who lands on it is the winner. To make the game more complicated, make each child stand on one leg when (s)he lands on the island — like a peg-leg pirate.

PIN THE TREASURE CHEST ON THE ISLAND

This is a variation of an old and popular game — 'Pin the Tail on the Donkey'. Other variations could be: stick a nose onto a clown's face, put the princess in the castle.

Props A blindfold, an island drawn onto stiff card with a cross marked on the spot where the treasure can be found, a small treasure chest also cut from card with a pin in it, a pencil.

To Play Each child in turn is blind-folded and carefully handed the treasure chest with the pin in it. S(he) has to pin the tail onto the island as near to the X as possible. Mark with a pencil the child's name at the place where the pin went into the drawing. Repeat with each child in turn — the one who is nearest the X wins.

THE GREAT FISH RACE

This is a team game which requires enough children to form two teams.

Props Two fish shapes cut from paper, and two rolls of newspaper.

To Play Line the children up in their teams at one end of the room and mark the other end with two chairs or cushions. Each child in turn has to flap the fish using the rolled up newspaper to the marker and back to the beginning. The rolled-up newspaper is then handed to the next person in the team to carry on doing the same. The winning team is the one who finishes first. If the fish is moved by hand, that person has to go back to the beginning and start again.

Papier-mâché fish make fun table decorations. You can have them lying around the table as though they have been stranded and then they make good going home presents. To make them, cut two fish shapes from card, staple the shapes together leaving a gap through which you stuff paper to fill them out. Cover the card with layers of papier-mâché (see page 10). Leave to dry in a warm place and then paint them with bright colours. Finally, paint on a coat of polyurethane.

A treasure chest can be made from a hinged tin or box. Spray it with gold paint and decorate with pretend paper money, coins and diamanté or stick-on sequin jewels. The coins can be made from colour photocopies or from magazines. Alternatively, rub onto thin paper over real coins. Silver bottle tops too can be put to use as coins. Fill the treasure chest with foil-covered chocolate coins or sweets wrapped in jewel-like coloured paper.

A Treasure Island Tablecloth

1 Make a tablecloth by painting waves onto a roll of lining paper or a bought white paper tablecloth.

2 Then either draw fish, boats, mermaids and a compass rose on separate pieces of paper, or photocopy the items from books, enlarge them and colour them in.

3 Stick them all onto the tablecloth.

Party Food

Pirates love to eat, drink and do all things in excess. When making the food for this party, have some fun creating pirate faces and the bones of his enemies!

SWEET PIRATE FACE BISCUITS

1 packet plain sweet biscuits
glacé icing, in several
    colours (see page 15)
miniature sweets such
    as jelly beans, jelly
    babies and miniature
    Liquorice Allsorts
sugar paste
food colouring

1 Paint the pirate features onto the biscuits using the glacé icing. Or make faces using the sweets, sticking them on with glacé icing.
2 From sugar paste cut out scarves and eye patches, paint with food colouring and also stick onto the biscuits using glacé icing.

THE BONES OF YOUR ENEMIES

2 tbsp tomato ketchup
2 tbsp brown fruity sauce
1 tsp soy sauce
1 tsp clear honey
¼ tsp french mustard
1 chicken drumstick per person
iceburg lettuce
cucumber
tomatoes
1 egg, beaten
brown food colouring
small pitta breads
tomato ketchup for serving

1 Mix the ketchup, brown sauce, soy sauce, honey and mustard together. Make cuts in the skin of the drumsticks and then coat with the sauce.
2 Cook under a pre-heated grill for 15 minutes, turning frequently.
3 Shred the lettuce and slice the cucumber and tomatoes. Mix the egg and a few drops of food colouring together and paint a skull and crossbones onto the pittas. Heat under the grill, split open the pittas and fill with the salad ingredients and top with the leg of your enemy. Add his blood in the form of tomato ketchup.

DEAD MAN'S FINGERS

25g (1oz) butter
225g (8oz) chopped
    dates
1 tbsp sugar
1 tbsp self-raising
    flour
1 egg

Pre-heat the oven to a temperature of 180°C (350°F, gas mark 4).
1 Melt the butter in a saucepan and add all the other ingredients.
2 Press the mixture into a 17.5-cm (7-in) greased baking tin. Cook for 30 minutes, remove from the oven and when it has cooled slightly, cut into fingers.

COCONUT ISLAND CAKES

quantity cake mix
    (see page 15)
25g (1oz) desiccated
    coconut
paper cake cases
glacé icing
    (see page 15)
green food colouring
110g (4oz) desiccated
    coconut
chocolate twigs
small quantity sugar paste,
    coloured green

Pre-heat the oven to a temperature of 200°C (400°F, gas mark 6)
1 Mix together the ingredients as on page 15 but add the desiccated coconut. Bake in the paper cases for 15 minutes.
2 When cool, decorate with glacé icing sprinkled with green coloured coconut grass, and add palm trees made of chocolate twigs and green sugar paste leaves.

A Sixties Disco Party

Even if you don't remember the sixties, you will have seen pictures and news clips of the era: long straight hair, kaftan dresses, loons and kipper ties were the fashions. Flowers and bells every- where, even drawn onto faces.

Costumes

- Sixties' wear was long flowing dresses, headbands and lots of flowers.
- Wear long Indian print dresses and skirts.
- Wear headbands decorated with paper flowers.
- Either wear your hair long or borrow an old wig (especially the boys).
- Lots of bead necklaces and bells should be worn around the neck.
- Lots of rings should be worn on your fingers.
- John Lennon glasses or sun glasses were cool.

- Kipper ties too were fashionable: find old versions or make them from card and add elastic to the knot.
- Tie dye tee shirts by wrapping cotton round them, placing them in dye, and then removing the string. A marvellous swirling pattern appears.
- To make loons or bell bottomed jeans, insert coloured sections in the sides of the legs.
- Dye Granddad vests purple or orange.
- Wear clogs.

For kipper ties (see photograph to the right) draw an extremely wide tie shape with a large knot at the top onto thin card. Cut it out. Thread shirring elastic long enough to go around the child's neck onto a needle and attach it at either side of the tie's knot. Decorate the tie with brightly coloured swirly patterns and flowers. Make the colours as lurid as possible — colours such as purple and orange or lime green and bright yellow were favourite combinations.

Sixties Decorations

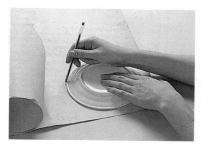

1 Draw around a side plate onto brightly coloured card. Cut out one circle per flower.

2 Cut petals from contrasting coloured papers, drawing around a template. Cut six petals per flower.

3 Stick the petals to the back of the circles.

Party Games

The games/activities suggested here are aimed at the 9 and above age groups who by this age are usually very knowledgeable about popular music.

DANCE ISLANDS

This is an active game which starts the party off with a swing.

Props Disco music (either taped or use a disc or CD), newspaper cut into circles — enough for half the number of guests and not too large.

To Play Spread the islands (paper) out on the floor with as much space as possible between each. Children dance to the music until it stops which is when they must get onto one of the islands. Each island must have two children on it and they must not fall off which means they will probably have to hold onto each other. Any child not on an island or who is unable to remain on one is out. Remove one island each time the music begins again. The couple remaining at the end, win.

GUESS THE SONG

This is a quieter game which requires concentration.

Props Tape recorder, tape with current pop songs — this can be prepared by you, in which case leave a gap between each opening line and the rest of the song or a shop-bought one. If you decide to use one that is bought, listen to the tape first and make a note of the number at which each song begins. Eight to ten songs are sufficient. Paper, pencils.

To Play Each child has a pencil and paper (ensure everyone has a hard surface or something to lean on). Play the first few bars of the first song then allow time for the players to work out the title of the song and then write it down. Replay this a couple of times if you think it necessary. While this is being written down, forward the tape to the next song. Play the next snippet and again allow everyone to write down the title of the song, and so on. All players pass papers to their right and they are marked. This game can also be played in teams which may be advisable depending on the knowledge of the children.

BALLOON POPPING

This is a fun, energetic game, good for using up a lot of energy!

Props Pop music (tapes, discs, CDs), balloons — enough for each child and a few extra.

To Play Each child is given a balloon which they hold in their hands. When the music starts, the balloon must be thrown gently in the air, hands must be held behind the back and the balloon has to be kept off the ground. This can be achieved by heading, lifting up the knees, kicking, nudging, etc. Any child who lets the balloon touch the ground is out. This continues until there is only one person left who is the winner. If the game becomes too chaotic at any stage, stop the music and begin again.

Party Food

The food for a disco party should be quite sophisticated to fit in with the concept of growing up. Easy-to-eat finger food is best, including chicken drumsticks, ribs, garlic bread, and pizza. Finish off the whole with peppermint creams.

CHICKEN DRUMSTICKS (see The Bones of Your Enemies, page 92)

SPARE RIBS (see Rustlers Ribs, page 86)

GARLIC BREAD (see Cowboys and Indians, page 86)

PIZZA

ready-made pizza base
tomato paste
salami slices
1 tomato, sliced
anchovies
olives
Cheddar cheese

Pre-heat the oven to a temperature of 220°C (425°F, gas mark 7)
Spread the tomato paste over the Pizza base. Cover the pizza in salami and tomatoes and then add the anchovies and olives. Grate the cheese on top and bake on a greased baking tray in the oven for 15 minutes.

PEPPERMINT CREAMS

1 egg white
225g (8oz) icing sugar
peppermint essence
green food colouring

1 Beat the egg white until stiff, sieve the sugar and gradually fold it into the mixture – only add enough sugar to make a firm paste and no more. Add three drops of essence into the mixture and a few drops of food colouring.
2 Sprinkle the work surface with icing sugar and roll out the paste until 6mm (¼in) thick. Cut with a tiny cutter and store in an airtight tin until ready to eat.

SPICED ALMONDS

3 tbsp sunflower seed oil
250g (9oz) flaked almonds
salt

Heat the oil in a pan, add the almonds and fry until golden brown. Drain on kitchen paper and sprinkle with salt.

DEVILS ON HORSEBACK

1 piece streaky bacon per devil
1 prune per devil
cocktail sticks

De-rind the bacon and wrap each prune in a piece of bacon secured with a cocktail stick. Grill for 4-5 minutes until the bacon is crisp.

Table Decorations

Flower power table-ware is a must. To decorate the food bowls, make long chains of brightly coloured flower petals. Use only half of a petal and join them so that the straight edge runs along the edge of the bowl. Fasten strips of petals around the tops of bowls and dishes using sticky tape on the underside of the strips. To decorate cups and straws, cut flowers and middles from card and stick to plain paper cups, and pipe cleaners to wrap round straws.

A tablecloth can be made by joining two pieces of lining paper down the centre so that the cloth covers the tea table. Draw large and small flowers all over in pencil. Add 'ban the bomb' slogans and yin/yang symbols. Colour everything in as appropriate. Sponge between the flowers and symbols with royal blue poster paint. If the paint overlaps too much, colour the flowers again. Add felt pen outlines.

Knights and Damsels

This is just the kind of party to bring out the best in people, with beautiful costumes, a chance to role play a gallant knight or a beautiful lady, or be a page boy or girl. Make wonderful costumes from metallic materials, and tiaras and crowns from cardboard covered in sweet papers and diamanté.

Costumes

- A damsel (see previous page) could wear a pointed conical hat made as described on page 73.
- For her top, criss-cross a vest bodice with ribbons and add a sequin at each intersection.
- A knight's shield is described to the right and a helmet overleaf.
- For a gold cape (see previous page), use gold fabric and add a drawstring 5cms (2ins) from the top to make a stand up collar.
- A glittery crown adds some glamour — see the description opposite.

A shield is basically made from the back of a large washing powder box. On the back of the box, draw an oval, round or heart-shaped outline and cut the shield out. Then cut the top off the box with the handle and stick this onto the back of the shield. To decorate the shield, either spray it with silver or cover in foil and then draw on a design and paint it with poster paints. You may wish to make up your own coat of arms or paint on the wearer's initials.

Party Games

It would be good to have medieval music playing as the guests arrive to create an atmosphere. If this is hard to find, the sound of one instrument playing a classical piece will be just as appropriate.

MEMORY TRAY

This is a quiet game which calms down proceedings before tea!

Props Tray with objects placed on it such as pencil, nut, banana, tissue, piece of lego, postcard, hole punch, sweet, ring, candle, etc. You also need a tea towel to cover the tray, pencils and paper — enough for each child.

To Play Give each child a piece of paper and pencil. (Make sure they all have somewhere to lean so writing is easy.) When all are seated and quiet, place the tray in the middle of the room where all can see it. Take the cover off the objects for one minute. No writing is allowed in this time. Replace the cover and then the children can start listing all the objects they can remember. When you judge that they have had enough time tell them to stop. You can then mark the papers or pass them around the room for the players to mark. The one who has the most correct answers, wins.

ROYAL SUIT

This game causes great hilarity and can be played several times.

Props Ace, King, Queen and Jack from all suits of a pack of cards. Ideally you need 12/16 children to play, but if the number of children is not divisible by four then play the game several times. One chair for each group of four.

To Play The chairs are lined up at one end of the room with a lot of space between each while children sit around the other sides of the room. The playing cards are shuffled and laid face down on the floor in the middle of the room. When you say 'Go' each child picks up a card. As soon as an Ace is picked up, that child quickly sits on one of the chairs and calls out the suit. The other children have to go the Ace of their suit and sit one on top of the other with the King on the Ace's lap, the Queen on the King's and the Jack on top. The first four to do this win.

STRUNG TOGETHER

This is a good, less boisterous, game.

Props Two long pieces of string.

To Play Children are divided into two teams with the first in line holding the piece of string. When the signal is given, the first child has to thread the string through his/her clothes from top to bottom. Once the string starts to appear the next player can start to feed it through his/her own clothes, but from bottom to top. This continues until all team members are strung together. The first team to be joined together wins.

Making a Glittering Crown

1 Cut a crown shape from cardboard. Stick splodges of wet tissue over the cardboard and then cover with layers of papier-mâché (see page 10).

2 Paint with white emulsion paint. Smooth out metallic sweet papers until they are flat and then stick them onto the nodules on the crown.

3 Paint the crown gold and then stick diamanté decorations all over it. Add patterns in silver pen. Thread elastic at the back to hold it on the head.

Headwear

A helmet is made with the ever faithful papier-mâché (see page 10) – this time over a balloon. Blow up a round balloon to a suitable size and then cover it with five or six layers of papier-mâché. When the papier-mâché is dry, pop the balloon and then cut away the front of the helmet to accommodate the face. Add a yogurt pot upside down to the top of the helmet. Cover the whole with another coat of papier-mâché, paint it silver and finally add a feather to the top.

A conical hat is cut from a square of card, as if making a witch's hat (see page 73). Before folding the hat into a cone shape, glue on a metallic fabric or spray with gold or silver. Cut a strip of net or a fine fabric and gather it round the bottom in swags and stick sequins on the front of the hat. Make a hole about the size of a ping pong ball at the top, cut a long piece of net and poke it into the top so it flows to the floor.

Party Food

The food for knights and their fair ladies has to be a banquet. Frosted fruits, medieval mead, shields on toast and swords in the stone are all food fit for the finest lords and ladies of the land.

ICE MAIDENS

soft-scoop ice cream
paper cake cases
ice cream cones
small sweets
glacé icing, coloured brown (see page 15)

Put one scoop of ice cream in each paper case. Put a cone on top, upside down. Make faces in the ice cream with two small sweets for eyes, one for the nose and another for the mouth. Make the hair with coloured glacé icing.

SWORDS IN THE STONE

900g (2lb) potatoes
1 sausage per person
butter
milk
1 pitta bread per person

1 Peel and boil the potatoes. Grill the sausages, turning as they brown. Take the potatoes off the heat, drain and mash with butter and milk. Grill the pittas till they puff out.
2 Fill each pitta with mashed potato and stick one sausage in the potato so that it is sticking out of the pitta like a sword.

CHEESE SHIELDS

1 cheese slice per person
1 slice of bread per person
red pepper, cut into thin strips
green pepper, cut into thin strips

1 Cut each cheese slice into four and place on a piece of bread with pepper strips between the quarters. Put under a hot grill until the cheese bubbles.
2 Cut the cheese on toast into a shield shape.

FROSTED FRUITS

grapes
apricots
plums
greengages, or any
    soft fruit in season
egg white
caster sugar

Paint each piece of fruit with egg white and then dip it in the caster sugar. Shake off the excess sugar and arrange the fruit on a glass cake stand.

MEDIEVAL MEAD

blackcurrant juice
hot water
sultanas
glass goblets

Mix the blackcurrant juice with hot water. Put some sultanas in the bottom of each glass and then add the hot juice.

A Dinosaur and Cavemen Party

This is a truly primitive party. To make the costumes, use scraps of fake fur or any brown fabric and for dinosaur masks, use card and the pointed parts of egg boxes. Decorate a table-cloth or lining paper with animal foot prints. Make caveman drawings for the walls of your cave!

Costumes

- Sew together piece of fake fur, suede, or real bits of leather using zigzag stitch to make a male or female cave costume.
- Use face paints to paint the face brown.
- A club is made by following the instructions to the right.
- Make a tooth necklace by making papier-mâché teeth (see page 10) and stringing them on a piece of string.
- Make a dinosaur body from a long length of green fabric, gathered at the neck with elastic. Cut armholes so the dinosaur can eat!
- Make a pterodactyl hood using the pattern on page 14 and attach felt spikes along the top.

Clubs are simply made by rolling a broadsheet newspaper into a tube, halving it and sticking the two pieces together with masking tape to make a handle. Blow up a small balloon and cover it with three layers of papier-mâché (see page 10). When the papier-mâché is dry, pop the balloon, cut a hole in the side of the club head and insert the handle. Fasten securely in place with masking tape and add another layer of papier-mâché over the top of the whole thing. Decorate the club with brown paint and then varnish with clear varnish.

Decorating the Cave's Walls

1 Crumple brown paper to give the natural uneven look of caves.

2 Sponge brown and terracotta paints over the drawings.

3 At last an opportunity for those who can only do stick drawings. Using fine black felt pens, draw stick men with spears onto brown wrapping paper.

1

2

3
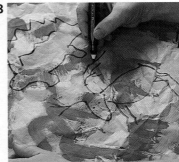

Party Games

SPIKE THE STEGOSAURUS

This is a good activity with which to begin as it occupies the children as guests arrive.

Props Large drawing of a stegosaurus pinned on a board, spikes drawn on individual pieces of paper, (one per child), drawing pins, two scarves.

To Play When guests arrive they are shown the drawing of the dinosaur and given a spike drawn on a piece of paper. S(he) writes their name on this and then waits his/her turn. Each child is blindfolded and turned round three times, left to face the board and given his/her spike to hold. S(he) must try to place this in the appropriate place on the stegosaurus's back. This is then pinned by you onto the board. The child then takes the blindfold off to see where it has been placed. When everyone has had a go, those children whose spikes are in roughly the correct place win.

THE DINOSAURS ARE HUNGRY!

This activity can be played at the same time as 'Spike the Stegosaurus' if you have enough helpers. 'The Dinosaurs Are Hungry' is really 'Bobbing Apples', and it is included to show how difficult it is to eat with no hands.

Props Three or more large bowls, three scarves, three or more waterproof macs/ aprons, apples/pears, towels.

To Play Fill the bowls half way up with water and place several apples into this. Dress three children in waterproofs as far as possible and loosely tie their hands behind their backs. On the word 'Go' the children have to kneel in front of a bowl and try to take a bite out of an apple. They keep attempting to do this until you think they have had enough. Three more children should be ready to take their places. Two children can use the same bowl if it is large enough but everyone can get very wet!

DINOSAUR TRACKING

This game is far better in a large open space where children can run, but if played inside let the dinosaurs crawl about.

Props Tape recorder, tape with music.

To Play Allocate three areas of the room, one for each type of dinosaur such as stegosaurus, brontosaurus and pterodactyl. Divide the children into roughly three equal groups calling them by the same names. Players then crawl around to the music imitating the way in which their dinosaur moves. As soon as the music stops the dinosaurs move as quickly as possible to the safety of their area. The last to reach the safety of home is out. Repeat this until one dinosaur is left and he/she is declared the winner.

RAMPAGING DINOSAURS

This game is not as rough as it sounds and it is great fun.

Props Miniature boxes of chocolate beans.

To Play Divide the children into teams of equal numbers and give each child in the team the name of the dinosaur. This means each team has one tyrannosaurus, one brontosaurus, one stegosaurus, one pterodactyl, etc. Everyone sits in one large circle, but with each team sitting next to each other. Place the box of chocolate beans in the middle of the circle. When you call out, 'Tyrannosauruses hunt for food', all those who are tyrannosauruses get up and run round the outside of the circle, back to their places, through the space where they were sitting and the first one picks up the chocolate beans. Everyone sits down again and the exercise is repeated as often as you wish calling a different type of dinosaur each time. At the end, the team with the highest number of beans wins. (Ensure each member of the winning team has a box of chocolate beans).

Party Food

If you wish is to gnaw on a bone or eat a volcano this is the party for you. We even have some cavemen rock cakes, and some miniature dinosaurs for you to make.

OLD BONES

3 spare ribs per child
bought barbecue sauce

Put the ribs under a hot grill and turn until brown. Take out and serve immediately with the barbecued sauce.

VOLCANOES

See the recipe for Coconut Ghosts (page 74), but replace the chocolate drops with red jam.

Make as for Coconut Ghosts, but when cooked dent the top of the volcano and pour on red jam.

SWAMP MUD

Coke
Vanilla soft-scoop ice cream

Pour the Coke into a tumbler and add a scoop of ice cream.

ROCK CAKES

225g (8oz) wholemeal self-raising flour
pinch of salt
½ tsp mixed spice
110g (4oz) butter or margarine
75g (3oz) brown sugar
50g (2oz) currants
1 egg, beaten
2 tbsp milk
rind of ½ a grated lemon

Pre-heat the oven to a temperature of 190°C (375°F, gas mark 5).
1 Mix all the dry ingredients together and add the margarine and beaten egg. Add enough milk to make a soft but firm dough. Place on a greased baking sheet in rocky mounds.
2 Bake in the oven for about 15 minutes, until just brown.

MARZIPAN DINOSAURS

1 packet marzipan
various food colourings

1 Divide the marzipan into several batches and colour each lot with a different food colouring (use only a few drops of each).
2 Mould small quantities into dinosaur bodies, add heads, feet and fat tails and then small, varied coloured, blobs down the backs to make the scales.

Table Decorations

Bone tableware is a fine addition to a party such as this. To make table mats, draw a large bone shape onto a sheet of card, paint in an off-white colour and cut it out as a table mat. Also draw bone shapes onto white paper cups and plates. For a three-dimensional and somewhat surprising effect, cover some old cutlery handles in papier-mâché strips (see page 10) and build them up until they look like real bones. Paint an off-white bone colour.

A volcano table centre can be made from a circle of chicken wire with a diameter of 48cms (18ins). Cut a 'V' from the edge of the circle to the centre so that the circle can be turned into a cone. Attach this cone to another flat piece of chicken wire using sticky tape. Remove the point from the top of the cone and replace it with a small circle, indented crater-style. Cover the whole volcano with papier-mâché (see page 10) and paint as grey and brown. When dry, add toy dinosaurs.

A Christmas Party

Christmas is a good time to
celebrate and have a party.
Costumes can be traditional
Father Christmas outfits,
or how about being one
of his reindeer? Make
pudding- or Christmas
tree-shaped table mats,
and make a Christmas
tree-shaped Christmas
cake and let the children
decorate it as garishly
as they like.

Costumes

- Make a holly and mistletoe headband, or a snowflake headband. Cut a snowflake from a folded circle of card and attach to the headband.
- A Father Christmas suit (see right and all-in-one pattern on page 12) with a hood can be made from red winceyette edged with white fake fur.
- For a Christmas tree costume (see right), use green fabric with a ridgeline hoop at the hem to make it stand out. Decorate it with lines of gathered netting, bells and tinsel.
- Make a headband from a cake surround with a glittery star attached to the front.
- A snowflake costume can be cut from white card, attached with straps and worn with a white tee shirt and tights or leotard.
- The Christmas tree fairy is made from a leotard with net skirt, silver wings and fur trim attached.

Room Decorations

A Christmas garland made from salt dough (see page 10) is simply made by rolling out two sausages of dough, twisting them together and placing around a plate to make a neat circle. Remove the plate and place the garland on a baking tray. Cut out holly leaves and berries and stick all over the dough using a dab of water. Stick a paper clip in the back of the garland for hanging and then bake until cooked (see page 10). Decorate with watercolours and a coat of clear varnish.

A Christmas pudding invitation is made by first folding a piece of brown card in half. For the base of the pudding, draw and then cut a rounded shape at the bottom of the card. For the topping, cut a yellow custard shape from yellow sticky paper and stick it onto the front of the card. Finally, cut green holly and red berries from sticky paper, put them onto cardboard, cut out the cardboard and stick it to the top of the pudding, above the custard, to create a good three-dimensional effect.

Paper chains, lanterns and streamers use masses of scraps of coloured paper. For paper chains, cut strips of Christmas paper and link them together. Make paper lanterns by cutting a piece of card 30 × 40cms (12 × 16ins) and folding it in half lengthwise. Make cuts at regular intervals from the fold to within 5cms (2ins) of the edge. Open out the lantern and stick the two sides together. Add a handle to the top. For streamers, cut strips of coloured crepe paper and twist together.

Party Games

Children are very excitable at this time of year so it is good to have quiet games interspersed with the noisier ones at this particular party.

CHOCOLATE BEAN SUCKING

This should produce a wonderful silence for a short time!

Props Straws, chocolate beans, empty plastic containers (one per child).

To Play Each participant is given a straw and an empty container. Everyone kneels in a circle and the chocolate beans are scattered on the floor. On the word 'Go', the beans have to be sucked up by sucking through the straw — no hands are allowed. No prize is necessary as everyone has more or less beans depending on how busy they have been.

THE MISSING PARTS

This game is about doing a jigsaw on the move and can be made more or less complicated depending on the age of the children.

Props Collect magazines/colour supplements and remove full-page pictures with a Christmas connection, one for each player. Carefully cut each picture into three parts using wavy or straight lines. Hide two parts around the house.

To Play Give the remaining pieces of each picture to each player who then has to find the missing pieces. If younger children are playing, make sure you give them the middle of the three parts. To make the game simpler, cut the pictures into two not three. The first one to find his/her picture wins.

CHOCOLATE RACE

This is good fun and can produce great hilarity.

Props Plate, knife, fork, gloves, scarf, hat, jacket, bar of cooking chocolate, dice, small table and chair.

To Play Children sit in a circle around the table and chair. Clothes are placed on the floor or back of the chair, the slab of chocolate is placed on the plate on the table with a knife and fork at either side. One child starts off by throwing the dice. If a six is thrown that child quickly runs to the pile of clothes, puts them all on, sits at the table and attempts to eat the chocolate by using a knife and fork. This can continue until the next player throws a six. The first child then has to take off the clothes while the next is putting them on before sitting at the table. This continues until all the chocolate has been eaten.

Christmas Pudding Mats

1 Draw the design onto paper and then cut out all the components — the pudding, custard, berries, holly, currants — separately. Pin the pattern pieces onto felt and cut each one out. Cut out two puddings.

2 Stick the custard onto one of the puddings.

3 Build up the rest of the design adding leaves, berries and currants. When the pieces are dry on the front, turn the design over and stick the other pudding onto the back to stiffen the mat.

Party Food

Christmas party food should be festive, in keeping with the season. For a party at this time of year, it is also fun to have food which can decorate the tree such as gingerbread shapes and sweet garlands.

GINGERBREAD COOKIES

110g (4oz) soft light brown sugar
90g (3oz) sunflower margarine
110g (4oz) golden syrup
275g (10oz) plain flour
2 tsp ground ginger
1 tsp bicarbonate of soda
glacé icing, white (see page 15)

Pre-heat the oven to a temperature of 180°C (350°F, gas mark 4)
1 Place the sugar, margarine and golden syrup in a saucepan and heat gently until the syrup melts, but is still only tepid. Sift the flour, ginger and bicarbonate of soda into the mixture and mix to a dough.
2 Roll the dough on a lightly floured board to a thickness of 6mm (¼in). Using appropriately shaped cutters, cut gingerbread men, Christmas trees and robins. Skewer a hole near the top of each, place on a baking tray and cook for 10-12 minutes or till deep golden brown. Decorate with glacé icing when cool.

MINATURE YULE LOGS

small chocolate swiss rolls
glacé icing, white
    (see page 15)
1 packet marzipan
green and red food
    colouring
2 chocolate Flakes

1 Cover the top of each log (swiss roll) in glacé icing.
2 Divide the marzipan into two: three quarters and a quarter. Mix the larger quantity with a few drops of green food colouring and the smaller quantity with a few drops of red food colouring.
3 Roll out the green marzipan and cut out holly leaf shapes and make holly balls with the red marzipan. Decorate each log with three leaves and a few berries. Break the Flakes into pieces and push them into the logs at random.

STAINED GLASS BISCUITS

175g (6oz) plain
    flour
110g (4oz) softened
    butter
50g (2oz) caster sugar
1tbsp milk
greaseproof paper
various shaped cutters
15 boiled sweets

Pre-heat the oven to a temperature of 180°C (350°F, gas mark 4).
1 Mix the flour and fat together, stir in the sugar and milk and mix to form a dough. Wrap in cling film and chill in the fridge for 15 minutes.
2 Roll out the dough to a depth of 6mm (¼in) and stamp out different shaped biscuits. Place each biscuit on the greaseproof paper. Using a small cutter remove a circle from the centre of each biscuit and replace it with a boiled sweet. Chill the biscuits for 30 minutes before baking for 20-25 minutes.
3 If you want to hang the biscuits on the tree, skewer a hole near the top of each one before baking. When the biscuits are removed from the oven you will need to remake the holes as they start to close up. When the biscuits are cold, peel them off the greaseproof paper, thread with red or green ribbon and hang.

SWEET NECKLACES

1 packet Jelly Tots
1 packet Jelly Babies
1 packet Fruit Polos
1 packet Mint Polos
1 packet biscuits with holes
1 packet small sweets
large darning needle
80cms (30ins) of embroidery thread per necklace

1 Thread the sweets and biscuits onto the needle and thread. Some of the sweets will need to be pierced with the needle first. When the needle gets sticky, clean it with a damp cloth.
2 When each thread is full, tie the ends together to make a necklace or hang it from the tree.

Index

Page numbers in *italics* represent photographs